PRAISE FOR STUART BRISCOE'S BOOKS

Stuart Briscoe is a master at finding the light switches, turning them on and exposing the life that is to be found in all Scripture. In the twelve chapters of his book *Taking God Seriously*, twelve prophets become twelve neighbors and friends, talking about things that concern us, our lives and our world today, with a diagnosis of our difficulties, and remedies to be applied. I suppose that's doing what prophets are supposed to do!

Charles Price
Senior Pastor, The Peoples Church, Toronto
Host of Living Truth television and radio

Taking God Seriously is a book that provides a refreshing window into twelve books of the Old Testament that are practically unknown by most Christians. Stuart brings the words of the ancient prophets into our daily lives with contemporary illustrations and insights into human nature combined with a firm grasp of what messages the prophets were trying to convey. This book challenges us to leave casual Christianity behind and take God seriously, just as the prophets did!

Dr. Erwin W. Lutzer, Senior Pastor
The Moody Church, Chicago, IL

With their own clear and practical biblical approach, Stuart and Jill Briscoe untangle the misunderstandings and mistakes that keep many Christians from enjoying the happiness of holiness. Read and apply their book, *Holiness without the Halo*, to your life and "the truth shall set you free" (John 8:32).

Warren W. Wiersbe
International Bible Teacher and Author
Lincoln, Nebraska

OTHER BOOKS BY THE AUTHOR

Holiness without the Halo

Taking God Seriously

GOD

Getting Into

Practical Guidelines for the Christian Life

Stuart Briscoe

CLC
PUBLICATIONS
Fort Washington, PA 19034

Getting Into God
Copyright © 2013 by D. Stuart Briscoe
All rights reserved. Published 2013

ISBN 13 (paperback):978-1-61958-152-4
ISBN (e-book): 978-1-61958-153-1

Published by CLC Publications

U.S.A.
P.O. Box 1449, Fort Washington, PA 19034

UNITED KINGDOM
CLC International (UK) 51 The Dean. Alresford, Hampshire, SO24 9BJ

Printed in the United States of America

This printing October 2013

Table of Contents

Introduction

Years ago I joined the Marines. Not out of choice, but compulsion. Arriving at the barrack gates, I found myself both elated and uneasy. The prospects of being a real live Marine were exciting to a young red-blooded kid who knew no better. And yet the strangeness of it all made me wonder. What would I have to do? Would I be able to do it? All the usual queries that accompany a new situation filled my mind.

The first few days served only to confirm my worst suspicions. I really had little idea of what was going on. Getting "kilted out" was one experience I will never forget. We were marched into a long shed which had a counter stretching the length of one wall. Behind the counter stood men who turned out to be geniuses. With scarcely a glance at us as we moved past, they estimated our size, tastes and abnormalities and, quicker than it takes to tell, they hurled piles of strange uniforms and equipment in our direction. We caught them as best we could and emerged from the shed "weary and heavy laden." Dispirited too. As we looked at our newly acquired possessions, it became clear to us that we had no idea what they were for, where they went, or what we were supposed to do with them. I didn't know whether to put them on my back, drape them round my neck, suspend them from my stomach, eat them, polish them, or salute them!

Christians sometimes get hit the same way. Having become excited about their new experience, they find themselves deluged with supplies and situations that are strange and vaguely disquieting. Big, black Bibles, shiny and obviously new. Hymnbooks full of strange tunes and strange expressions describing "rocks of ages," "fountains of blood" and "showers of blessing." Prayer lists of "the Lord's servants" somewhere on "the mission field" who "covet our prayers."

Terminology was a problem in those early Marine days, too. We were told to develop "esprit de corps." Now, I had "learned" French for six years (which was about six years more than most of my new friends), and I had little idea what they were talking about. You can see how enlightened the rest of the group was! Phrases were repeated with great solemnity, but one had the distinct impression there was not too much communication involved. For instance, one instructor insisted that we learn the phrase "to facilitate fragmentation," which was the answer he required to the question, "Why does a hand grenade have grooves?"

The terms to which a Christian must come are no less confusing. In Christian circles where there are no men and women, just "brothers" and "sisters," people don't get sick, they are "afflicted." They don't die, they are "called home." To uninitiated ears, "the will of God" and "the Word of God" sound almost the same, apostles and epistles tend to get mixed up and the difference between First and Second Chronicles and First and Second Corinthians can easily be missed.

However, in all fairness, I must say that determined efforts were made to see that we young Marines began to understand the terms and find out where all the equipment fitted. In due time we began to function properly, and for this I was grateful.

The design of this book is to do something similar for Christians, both new and not so new, who feel a need for instruction in some basic practicalities of Christian experience. Its aim is to help us get into God.

Before we go further, a word about being a Christian seems necessary. As the name implies, a Christian is related in some way to Christ. He or she belongs to Christ, is identified with Christ in much the same way that an Asian is related to Asia or a musician is identified by his music. Christ being who He is, there is no difficulty seeing that mere humans are highly privileged to have a relationship with Him—the eternal Son of God. They also accept the fact that the relationship must be on His terms and not theirs.

Herein lies a problem for some people. They feel they can be Christian without relating to Christ on His terms. So they profess Christianity but know little of what Christ taught, less of what He promised and even less of what He requires. Professions of this order are highly suspect and should be carefully scrutinized by all concerned.

Christ taught that the Father had sent Him into the world to bring people to an experience of God which they once enjoyed and subsequently lost. To do this, it was necessary for Him to die on the cross for sin, be buried to show the reality of His death and to rise again from the dead as a demonstration of God's acceptance of His sacrifice and an illustration of the extent of His victory over sin, death and hell.

It was on the basis of this teaching that Christ was free to make His demands. First, He demanded repentance. He left no illusions in people's minds as to what He felt about sin and how He expected people to call sin sin and turn from it. Then, He insisted on faith—faith and dependence that stopped trusting anything or anyone but Himself for blessing and meaning. Third, He talked forcefully of repentance and faith becoming visible in terms of commitment to Him and what He was do-ing—the kind of commitment that would gladly acknowledge and accept His authority. A commitment like that of the centu-rion's soldiers, who would go where he said to go and do what he told them to do and come when they were told to come (see Luke 7:8). All this "coming" and "going"—not to mention the "doing"—is demanding, for it can mean going where you don't want to go and doing what you have no desire to do and coming to Him when there are other things you prefer to do at that time.

But there is a resource to help in these difficult situations: the Holy Spirit. It is He—the third member of the Trinity—who lives within the repentant, dependent, committed Christian. He is there to stimulate, clarify, strengthen, encourage and, where necessary, prick. His function is to keep the Christian moving along in experiences ever-leading into deeper discoveries of what God wants to do. But besides this remarkable spiritual resource, God has given us many helps, pieces of equipment, practical aids, "means of grace." Call them what you will, so long as you use them. The Bible, prayer, fellowship, the church in all her functions—all are intended to aid the Christian in being what he became a Christian to be.

Now, I have no doubt that each of us is aware of these helps to spiritual living and growth. It would be difficult for us not to be aware, if only because of the Madison Avenue kind of ap-proach that uses slogans to alert us to some of these things.

"No Bible, no breakfast" was a favorite of Bible study pun-dits. But while the sentiment is admirable, there is no escaping the fact that most people find toast and tea more to their taste early in the morning than Timothy and Titus. This preference may be interpreted as lack of spirituality in some quarters, but this is hardly fair. It is more likely evidence of the fact that the person concerned has not been taught the necessity of daily Bible study and the advantages of doing it regularly early in the day.

Or how about "Seven prayerless days make one weak." The truth of that statement is beyond dispute. So is its convicting power! Even the most chloroformed conscience will feel something when confronted with that one! But I submit that is all it will do—make people feel guilty and uncomfortable. It is not designed to teach the how and the why and the when of prayer. Yet it is exactly in these areas that I believe most people need and desire help.

Have you seen "What's missing in CH__CH?" "UR!!" Clever, isn't it? But though it may well be true, it is doubtful that approach will have the noninvolved standing in line to get in next Sunday. Moreover, there is a distinct possibility that if people were taught what Christ meant by the church and were shown how and where they would fit in the church, they would be there. Involved and excited.

But I have reserved the worst till the last. We used to hear, "Put a tither in your tank." The phrase is a bit of wordplay referencing an advertising tagline for Exxon gasoline. For my money that was the all-time low. It degrades the beautiful concept of stewardship, confirms many of our critics' views of our mercenary outlook and probably doesn't get too many in the baptismal tank either. Skinflints don't become tithers that way, and people are not taught the joys of giving and the blessings of sacrificial commitment in that fashion. Yet so many are ready to learn if they get the chance.

Enough of my hang-ups about slogans. My intention is neither to knock down what others are doing or even to just knock. Rather, my desire is to build up and encourage people to press on in their relationship with the Lord, both by enunciation of principles found in Scripture and in practical suggestions concerning putting the principles into operation. So here goes. Let's get into God.

Part I

GETTING INTO
BIBLE STUDY

1

The Tools
of Bible Study

Recently I joined the local library which had just opened. The woman who assisted me was proud of the new facility and offered to show me around. As I was in a hurry, I declined and insisted I could find my way around, get the material I needed and be on my way. But it might have been wiser to accept her offer, for when I got among the well-stocked shelves, I needed help finding what I wanted.

Which brings me to the Bible! Whatever else the Bible is, it is a library. In fact, if you like statistics, you may be interested to know it contains 66 books, 1,189 chapters, 23,214 verses and 773,692 words in the King James Version. That amounts to a lot of places in which to get lost. And that is exactly what many people have done. So let's be practical about Bible study and see if we can get some ideas about really benefiting from it.

First, you have to be motivated. You have to want to study the Bible. Unfortunately, some people haven't even come this far. They assume that listening to a sermon once in a while is all that is necessary, but they are wrong. It is important that each Christian learn how to feed himself from the Word of God.

A few years ago, friends invited me to go to the opera. As I was their guest and they had a box for a performance of *Eugene Onegin*, I was happy to go with them. But it wasn't the greatest evening I ever spent. The leading soprano was a formidable-looking lady who sang in such a way that she seemed to intimidate completely the rather small tenor who was supposed to sweep her off her feet. Added to this, the opera was sung in Polish and Russian (so I was told!), for it was being performed in the Opera House in Prague, Czechoslovakia. Frankly, I got a little bored and I would have been happy to have quit after the first act because I had no idea what was happening. People are rarely motivated toward that which they don't understand. And I believe that many people are not motivated to the Bible because they don't understand its significance and importance. Let me point out to you four important facts concerning the Bible.

Fact No. 1—The Bible is inspired by the Holy Spirit. This means He, a member of the Holy Trinity, took time to move people to write what He wanted them to write so we would know what God thinks (see 2 Pet.1:21; 2 Tim. 3:16.) Most things we know are the product of man's research or thinking. But man has been proved wrong quite a few times, so we all know we have to treat his findings with care. If only God would tell us what's going on! Then we could have some degree of confidence and build our lives on what God said instead of the shaky ground of what man thinks. This is exactly what God has done in the Bible. Many times you read in it phrases like, "Thus says the Lord . . ." or "He spoke with authority . . ." or "Hear what the Spirit says. . . ." This is exciting, for it means that people living on a tiny planet in the twenty-first century can know what God thinks about things and what He plans to do.

Fact No. 2—The Bible is the only means of knowing how to be reconciled to God. Many people know something about

Him and would urgently like to know Him better than they do. But their knowledge is fuzzy, and they don't know which way to go or where to start looking for information. Paul said it is the Scriptures that make us "wise for salvation." That being the case, saved people should be highly motivated to research all they can about salvation in the only place they can find the information.

Fact No. 3—The Bible is the only place where you can get information on what to do after you have made a start in the Christian life. "Where do we go from here?" is a popular query and sad to say, some of the answers given are not too good. The same Bible passage that tells us it is inspired and makes us wise about salvation also tells us we need the Bible to become "complete and equipped." I am speaking of 2 Timothy 3:15–17. These verses also give us a few insights as to how the maturing and equipping take place: through teaching, reproof and correction. Teaching tells you what to do; reproof tells you what not to do; correction tells you what to do when you have done what you were told not to do. Which covers just about everything!

Fact No. 4—What is going to happen in the future? More and more people are studying horoscopes, visiting mediums and watching "world's end" movies because of an almost morbid interest in the future. But there is only one authoritative voice about the future—the Bible. In the Bible alone can we know what lies ahead, what the world is coming to, what happens after death, if there is an afterlife. The best man can produce is speculation; the Bible offers revelation. Speculation is the sum of what man thinks might happen; revelation is God's statement of what will happen!

There we have four big facts about the Bible which, when understood, become four big motivating factors. Of course, there are many others, but we'll settle for these four as sufficient to lead you to read, mark, learn and inwardly digest it, as *The Book of Common Prayer* says. If you have not been moved to do this till now, I hope you will change.

Second, you need some materials. Atop the list must obviously come the Bible itself. I am amazed by people who don't seem to think the Bible is necessary for their study of it. They remind me of the Welshman who, when the ball was lost in the middle of a fiery rugby match, said, "Don't bother about the ball. Get on with the game." There's as much chance of a good Bible study experience without a Bible as there is of a good rugby match without a ball!

In the English-speaking world we have so many editions of the Bible (both online and in print) to choose from that some people become confused. Two basic kinds of versions are available—those that seek to be a strict translation of the original Greek and Hebrew texts and those that give the sense by way of paraphrase. I have copies of both kinds and use them both. The difference between the paraphrase and translation is rather similar to the difference between a photograph and a watercolor sketch. The photograph is exact in every detail, while the sketch captures the truth of the subject without all the detail. The paraphrase type of Bible is often easier to read than the more strict translation, so I use the former for general reading and the latter for detailed study. The former gives me the overview of what the Bible is saying, but the latter gives me material from which I can make a careful study.

Which should you have? I recommend a copy of the Living Bible for general reading and either a King James Version (he didn't write it, but he did commission its translation in 1611 and, though it is old, it's great!) or the English Standard Version or New International Version for study.

There are many others, but we'll settle for those for now. Also, it's important to note that you can find online or via smartphone and tablet applications numerous translations of the bible as well as the concordances and commentaries discussed later.

The important thing about your Bible is that if you are going to study it, the print must be big enough. This is an elementary point, but necessary, because many Bibles have apparently been designed more for beauty than use. It also helps if there is a margin in which to make some notes, and you may even wish to invest in a loose-leaf Bible. This is designed, as its name suggests, with all its pages removable—not so you can get rid of the bits you don't like without spoiling your Bible, but so you can write lots of notes on the paper provided and then fit them in at the right place!

It is not always necessary to purchase a large, expensive new Bible. There are usually many available in old secondhand bookstores, and you can buy a half-dozen quite inexpensively. Then you can give some to your friends and get them studying, too!

Next, you need a notebook. Unless you have a loose-leaf Bible, you will need something in which to keep the products of your study. Nothing ornate is required; in fact, the simpler the notebook, the better. The point of the notebook is first of all to preserve your great thoughts and great discoveries. But there are other reasons. Have you ever noticed how easy it is to read something without thinking about it? You can't do that if you are taking notes, because you have to think what to write down as you are reading it. If, when you are through reading, there is a blank page looking at you from your notebook, you know something is wrong and you go back until you have something to record.

You may find it helpful to mark each page with the day's date and enter something daily! This is one of the best ways I know of keeping to daily reading, because it gets embarrassing to see nothing entered from June 1 to July 13! The notebook speaks! Moreover, it is always good to be able to look back over the years and see how your understanding has grown.

Then, you must have a concordance. This is an expanded index of the Bible. It lists every word in the Bible alphabetically, and under each word a reference is given for every place that word occurs. This is clearly helpful. Suppose you wanted to show someone how much God loved the world, but you couldn't remember John 3:16. You could turn to the word love and look at every reference until you found it. There is another good thing about a concordance. If you start looking under love, you will be amazed at how many times the word is used and you might just curl up on the rug with your Bible, notebook and concordance and do a study on the subject.

There are various styles of concordances. Some Bibles have a small one in the back next to the maps, or you can buy a large one in print. You can also generally find online versions of concordances that can be downloaded to your phone or tablet. The most famous are *Young's*, *Strong's* and *Cruden's*. Sometimes people ask me which would be best for them. I usually tell them, "If you're young, Young's; if you're strong, Strong's; and if you're crude, Cruden's. Personally, I have a Cruden's and my wife a Young's!"

You also need a box of colored pencils. These can be used to draw pretty pictures on the church bulletin during boring sermons, but this is not their primary use! I have found it helpful to have a system of marking my Bible, not only as a means of making things stick in my memory as I mark them, but also as a means of finding information at a later date. Now, don't get carried away at this point. There is a limit to the number of colors available, so you have to limit your system to relatively few subjects. The idea is to have a different color stand for each topic. In my study, I use red to mark things relating to salvation, blue for things relating to Christian experience, green for the Holy Spirit, black for everything relating to sin and judgment, orange for heaven and the life to come, brown for God the Father and terracotta for the Son.

There is nothing magic about this system, but it certainly is helpful. One day I arrived at a church to discover I was advertised to give a talk on "the Holy Spirit in Galatians." That was great except nobody had told me. Nevertheless, I was not left helpless. I just looked for the green lines neatly drawn under every reference to the Holy Spirit and explained each passage to the people.

When you mark your Bible, don't try to make it look like a Pollock painting. The less color, the better, as long as a neat line is drawn under the relevant words so you see the markings easily. Another suggestion is to do them in pencil, not in ink. The reasons for this are, first, the ink may go through the paper, and second, whenever you turn to a page of your Bible, you tend to look at the uninspired notes before the inspired text. If you have made your notes in ink, you might spend twenty years reading the same thing every time you turn to a particular page. If, however, you have made your notes in pencil, you will discover that the notes gradually wear away and by the time they do, it's time you thought of something new!

The materials I have listed are minimum requirements: Bible, notebook, concordance and pencils. You may wish to add to these minimum tools, and if so, I recommend a Bible dictionary. There are numerous ones available, ranging from small, compact books like *Halley's Bible Handbook* through the comprehensive *New Bible Dictionary* up to the five-volume set called *The Zondervan Pictorial Encyclopedia of the Bible*. Have a good look at some of these books whenever you get the chance, and you will soon see how valuable they are to a fuller understanding of the Bible.

Then, you may want to purchase a one-volume commentary on the Bible. You can start building your library of commentaries, with the *New Bible Commentary* or *Jamieson, Fausset and Brown's Commentary* or *Matthew Henry's Commentary*. Most of these are available online or via various bible apps. Some of these are more detailed than others and, of course, some are older than others. Old Matthew Henry has been around a long time (the commentary was initiated in 1704), but he still has much to say of great value, and if you like quaint language with your study you'll enjoy Henry!

A word of warning: Dictionaries and commentaries are supposed to be aids to study, not substitutes for study. Some people can't be bothered to dig for themselves; they just look for what someone else has found out and use that. Don't fall into this kind of trap. You will benefit more from the things you discover for yourself than from reading what someone else has said, but you will need the material of gifted teachers when you can't understand what the Scriptures mean at some points. That is the time to use your dictionary or commentary.

Shortly after I became a pastor, a woman asked me a question about the Bible which I could not answer. I said in reply, "I haven't the remotest idea." One of my most frequent answers! She was somewhat taken aback and then said, "Would you find out for me, please?" She was more taken aback when I said, "No." I explained that I would have to research it and she was as capable of doing that as I was, and furthermore, if she researched it herself, it would be much more meaningful to her and she could give the information to me. The next week she told me she had not been very pleased with me but, nevertheless, had done what I suggested. The result was that she really became enthusiastic about her own study. When a friend of hers asked her a question, she told her what I had said and they both got into their Bibles for themselves. We must not be lazy about our study and whenever possible must come up with some answers ourselves after gleaning all we can from the material available.

Having mentioned motivation and materials, I will talk about methods. Before doing that, however, I must say something important. Some things are so important to our approach to Bible study that if they are missing, even the finest methods in the world will not make our study profitable. The first of these things is our attitude toward the Scriptures. Some people approach the Bible as a masterpiece of literary achievement, which it certainly is. Others love its poetry and so they should, and still others revel in its historical detail and well they might. But the Bible will yield little of lasting value if it is approached purely as a literary or historical document. What really counts is the attitude that study of the Word of God leads us into truth. Yes, there is literary beauty. Yes, there is historical data. But above all this, there is eternal truth to be found nowhere else. Therefore, the approach of both the most learned theologian and the most humble Bible reader must be one of reverent anticipation that God will speak through the pages to the reader.

This leads naturally to the second point. When you study, pray. Ask the Holy Spirit who inspired the Word of God to interpret it to your own understanding. I know of no better prayer with which to approach the study of the Bible than "Open my eyes, that I may behold wondrous things out of your law" (Ps.

119:18 ESV).

2

How to Study a
Book of the Bible

Many books have been written about methods of Bible study: it is a big subject. In this book I will provide suggestions only for some prominent ones.

First, choose a short book and read it. Then read it again. If you have two versions of the Bible, read first one and then the other. When you have read it through two or three times, you will begin to be familiar with its overall content; think of a title you would give the book. After that, you should read the book through and look for its natural divisions. These divisions can be discovered by careful attention to the subject matter. When the subject matter changes, then, of course, you can detect the division.

Sometimes parts are introduced by words like "but" or "nevertheless" or "therefore." These words are often overlooked when people study their Bibles, but to overlook them is to miss the point of much of Scripture. For example, the word "but" shows the other side of the situation from the one just presented. Accordingly it introduces a new thought to the reader. Or take the word "therefore." It's often been said, "Whenever you see the word 'therefore,' ask yourself 'what's it there for?'" Good advice!

It is usually there to apply what has just been said. When the Bible teaches a great truth, it often says, "Therefore do such and such a thing." This is clearly something important. As you go on in your studies you will discover more of these important words that seem at first to be so unimportant.

There is still more involved in dividing the passage into its natural divisions! When you have done this, give each division a title of your own choosing. This will help to fix it in your mind and give you a brief summary of the contents of the passage.

Then look at each of these divisions with your title in mind and make a note of everything the passage says about the subject you have decided is the central point. For example, when I was a young man, I was transferred to a new town by the bank that employed me. Feeling a little strange, I checked into my hotel on the first day and settled down to read my Bible. As it happened, that day I turned to Psalm 1. I read it through two or three times and was struck by the fact that the psalm is basically a description of a "blessed man." I knew that "blessed" meant "happy," so I wrote in my notebook "The Happy Man." You can see what an exciting study this was for me at that time! I looked for the natural divisions and gave each one a title relating to the happy man. My notebook soon looked something like this:

THE HAPPY MAN—PSALM 1

1. His path . . . three things he avoids—verse 1
2. His pleasure . . . meditation in God's law—verse 2
3. His position . . . like a tree by the river—verse 3a
4. His productivity . . . bringing forth fruit—verse 3b
5. His progress . . . his unwithering leaf (ever-green) —verse 3c
6. His prosperity . . . whatever he does—verse 3d
7. His peace . . . the Lord knows his way—verse 6

You will notice that I suffer from alliteration, but you mustn't let this bother you. Sometimes it helps to have the different points begin with the same letter and sometimes they won't fit that way however hard you try! This is what I call a skeleton outline, and as bodies are nicer than skeletons, it is necessary to put flesh on the bones. Take the first point—"His path." Note three things that verse one says about the path of the "happy man", and you should spend time pondering these.

I have given an example from the Psalms that may prompt you to start a study of that book. This may be a little long for you, and you may become discouraged before it is completed, but at least you could work on a few Psalms.

On the other hand, you might like to try Philippians. I'll give you a start with the first chapter. When I began to study this chapter, I observed that Paul talked a lot about himself. That was exciting to me because I had been so enthralled with Paul I wanted to know as much as possible about him. So my notes were as follows:

PAUL WITH THE LID OFF—PHILIPPIANS 1

1. vv. 1–2   Greeting
2. vv. 3–8   Paul's delight
3. vv. 9–11   Paul's desire
4. vv. 12–21   Paul's devotion
5. vv. 22–26   Paul's dilemma
6. vv. 27–30   Paul's demands

I began to fill in the details under each heading and a profitable study followed.

How to Study a Word

It is a long step from a book to a word, but to study a chapter, phrase, or sentence is to come eventually to a word study. This is much more interesting and important than it sounds at first. If you look back at the outline I gave you for the first chapter of Philippians, you will note that I called the first two verses "Greeting." "Nothing very interesting there," you decide. "Let's get on with verse three." But look again. A number of words there deserve close scrutiny.

1. Servants
2. Saints
3. Overseers or Bishops
4. Deacons
5. Grace
6. Peace

I am sure you know what all those words mean, but do you perceive the depth of meaning in each of them? Let's take the word bondservant. First look in your concordance or Bible dictionary to find the meaning in the biblical sense. *Young's Concordance* says servant is a translation of the Greek word *doulos* which also means slave. Think of that! The word Paul uses to describe himself is the word slave. He thinks of himself as Christ's slave!

Or how about the word saint: most people think a saint is someone in a stained-glass window with a thing like a dinner plate behind his head. Look in your reference book. *Young's Concordance* says the Greek word *hagios* means saint, set apart, separate, holy. Nothing to do with dinner plates or windows. A saint is someone really set apart for God.

The word grace is such a remarkable word that whole books have been written about it. It is one of the great words of our faith, and I must restrain myself or I will stop writing about Bible study and finish up writing about grace. Studying this kind of word takes a long time. But it is time well spent. Check in your concordance every verse where the word occurs. Look up each verse and write down one thing the verse says about grace. When you have done this, you should have a good grasp of what grace is. And I'll warn you it is a lot of things—and every one of them is beautiful.

Having given you a few clues about looking into some of the words in the first two verses of Philippians 1, take another look at the verses and see the things we didn't mention. There are words so familiar, we didn't even notice them. But dare we overlook them? The words we left out are these:

1. Christ
2. Jesus
3. God
4. Father
5. Lord

Every one of these words is important, and you should look at all of them. Remember that all we have done is look into two verses which didn't seem important at all in the first place. This gives you some idea of what Bible study holds for those who will work at it.

How to Study a Character

When Oliver Cromwell was having his portrait painted, he said that for it to be realistic he should be shown "warts and all." In fact, he said he would not pay Mr. Lely, the artist, a "farthing" if he failed to do this.

I think the Holy Spirit was given similar instructions from the Father when He was commissioned to paint the portraits of biblical characters. Most of them are shown to be real people with real problems and in some instances they were shown to sink into deep sin. Yet God worked on them and did great things in their lives. For this reason I believe all Christians should engage in a study of biblical characters—because they can see what God can do with ordinary people.

There's another reason, too. Some Christians seem to think God did remarkable things with people like Peter and Paul because they were abnormal men. Saints stuck on plaster plinths! But this is not true, and I believe the Word of God is at great pains to show us it is not true. These persons were weak, failing people like us; nevertheless they had experiences that were superb. And so may we, for we have the same God.

To make a character study, first decide which figure interests you. Paul or David will rank high on everyone's list, but I suggest it is not wise to start with either. There is so much information about them, you might get lost in it. How about Stephen? He was a great man who made a tremendous impact and did it briefly! Turn to Stephen in your concordance and read everything the Bible says about him. All the information about Stephen is found in the book of Acts and most of it in chapters six through eight. So it isn't difficult to get the details together. When I studied him I noticed:

1. What he was, was irreproachable.
2. What he did was irrefutable.
3. What he said was irresistible.

You might look up the verses that give this information. Then look through Acts 6 and find one word that is used to describe Stephen. It occurs in connection with the following:

1. The Holy Spirit
2. Wisdom
3. Faith
4. Grace (translated "faith" in the King James)

5. Power

When you have found that word, you have found the secret of Stephen!

Then you might like to try Timothy, Silas, Mark, Jabez (yes, Jabez), Hannah, Mary, Ananias (both of them—be careful not to confuse them!) and when you're ready, do Peter!

The approach is the same for all of these characters, whether we know much or little about them. Find out everything the Bible says concerning them. Put it together in orderly form, perhaps by asking yourself some questions. The five W's are as good a form as any.

1. Who . . . was he?
2. What . . . did he do, say, think, desire?
3. Where . . . did he do what he did?
4. Why . . . was he the person he was?
5. Whom . . . did he affect by his life?

I must stop. If I go on any longer, you won't have time for your Bible study tonight and that would be self-defeating!

Part II

Going Deeper Into Prayer

3

What Is Prayer?

I once preached in the famous The Peoples Church in Toronto, Canada. After the meeting, an elderly lady came up to me, took my hand, kissed it and whispered, "I have prayed for you every day since you first preached in this church." Then she walked away before I had an opportunity even to ask her name. Old ladies rarely kiss my hand, but they may do it any time if they tell me they pray for me daily! I love old ladies who pray!

"But I'm not an old lady," you say. Well, just pray anyway because, though it must be admitted that some of the world's greatest praying people are old or infirm, or both, prayer is a vital part of every person's spiritual experience. I think it is no coincidence that young people and active types have more difficulty with prayer than older and less active people. You see, activity-prone people tend to find quietness, meditation and a "sweet hour of prayer" decidedly onerous and little more than a nice idea. The young and the active have a tendency to be self-sufficient and this militates against prayer. If youth, health and vigor keep you from prayer, then youth, health and vigor are not all they are said to be. They are robbing you of a precious part of your life.

Having said this, I admit I probably have more difficulty

with prayer than any other area of Christian experience—so I am going to read this chapter carefully when it is completed! Because of this difficulty, I have given considerable thought and study to the whole subject, and I hope the results of this study may be of help to you if you have any problems on this matter. I suspect you may have, because most Christians I talk to about their problems put prayer high on the list of their failings and deficiencies.

I'm sure that you have read of the great prayer warriors of the faith. There is George Mueller, who ran that fantastic orphanage in Bristol, England, on the basis of prayer. He used to sit the kids down to eat and lead them in thanksgiving for the food, without there being a crumb on the table! But the food had a habit of arriving in response to prayer. He never asked for a penny or a crumb for his kids, but he lacked nothing for them. He attributed it all to effective prayer.

Or David Brainerd, the missionary to the Native Americans, who prayed so hard and long under the trees of the forest that though the weather was cool, he was covered with a cold sweat.

Or John Wesley, the inimitable traveling preacher, who abhorred wasted time to such a degree that he read as he rode, with the horse's reins hanging loose on its neck. He regarded five o'clock in the morning as the best time to preach, and he complained when he was eighty-five that he couldn't walk or run as he once was able. Wesley was a man of prayer. In his "Scheme of Self-examination" he wrote, "Have I prayed with fervour? At going in and out of church? In the church? Morning and evening in private? Monday, Wednesday and Friday with friends? At rising? Before lying down? On Saturday noon? At the time I was engaged in external work? In private . . ."

No doubt you have heard of these men and others like them

and quite probably you have been convicted and become discouraged. "How on earth can I pray like that and still make a living in today's society?" you may have thought. So you may have decided that prayer is for those who are "inclined that way" and for you when you feel like the small boy who said, "I pray when I want something and I think there is no other way of getting it." Let's start at the beginning and make sure that we understand prayer clearly. What exactly is prayer? The poet James Montgomery said,

> Prayer is the soul's sincere desire,
> Uttered or unexpressed;
> The motion of a hidden fire,
> That trembles in the breast. [1]

That's beautiful, but you may be tempted to say, "Yes, but what is it?" Well, Montgomery added that prayer is "the Christian's vital breath" and his "native air." Magnificent imagery, but perhaps we need more practical answers. I believe we have been too mystical and poetic about prayer. Because it is a strange exercise of the human soul, we have tended to keep it delightfully vague, carefully couched in antiquated language and liberally peppered with clichés.

To me, prayer is the talking part of a relationship. We all know what it is to have a relationship with a wife or husband, child or parent, employer or employee. We all know how necessary it is that there be some verbal communication between participants in the relationship. An early sign that a marriage is going wrong is the lack of communication between husband and wife. One of the best ways to ensure that families fall apart is for parents and kids to routinely avoid talking to each other. And without a doubt, a surefire method of driving a business to bankruptcy is to have no means of communicating from "boss" to "bossed" what "boss" wants "bossed" to do.

The Bible provides numerous pictures of the Christian experience. The portrayal of it as a relationship is among the most helpful. We are Christ's friends (see John 15:15), His servants (see Col. 3:24) and His bride (see Rom. 7:4). Prayer is the talking part of these relationships: friend talking to friend, servant talking to master, bride talking to spouse.

If that is a valid definition of prayer, then I think we should be able to rid ourselves of some of the mystique that clouds our prayers and get down to praying more effectively.

Why Should I Pray?

The first reason why we should pray is to develop our spiritual relationship. This has been partially dealt with in the previous chapter. Relationships that don't talk don't grow. To say it another way, prayer is vitally important to the preservation and development of a relationship with the Lord. If you want the relationship to progress, it is obvious that prayer is a necessary activity.

But we must not fail to mention that conversation is usually two-way. It is important that prayer be seen in this light. "What," you may ask, "is the talking part of the Lord? How does He talk in prayer?" Strictly speaking, He does not converse, but He does talk through the Scriptures.

Thus Bible reading and prayer go together. The former is the Lord talking to you and the latter is your response or reaction. I am not saying you can pray only immediately after reading the Bible. But I definitely believe the effectiveness of your prayer life is closely related to your depth in the Scriptures.

And, of course, it is true to say that the effectiveness of your Bible study can be largely determined by your prayer life. Conversations that only have one talker aren't conversations—they are monologues. The Lord's talking through Scripture to you and getting no response of prayer is not likely to build a relationship. Neither is your doing all the talking and ignoring the fact that He reserves the right to speak. So the first reason why we should pray is to clarify and develop the intricacies of our relationship with the Lord.

The second reason why we should pray is that we have been told to! I just turned to my concordance, looked up the word pray and came up with the following:

> "PRAY for those who persecute you" (Matt. 5:44).
> "PRAY to your Father who is in secret" (6:6).
> "PRAY the Lord of the harvest to send out laborers" (9:38).
> "Watch and PRAY" (26:41).

All these references come from Matthew's Gospel. There was no need to look any further, for these commands to pray follow each other in quick succession.

Now, this brings a whole new dimension to prayer. Sometimes people think they don't need to pray because they don't like it, in the same way that they don't eat oysters because they're slippery. Whether they like it or not is irrelevant. They have been told to do it—Pray, that is! Others feel they are too busy to pray and therefore feel quite happy not praying. But it must be said that if they are too busy to do what they have been told to do, they are too busy doing some things they were not told to do or told not to do! Do you see what I mean?

Still others don't know how to pray and never take the time to find out, and accordingly, they never do it. Again, they are in serious trouble, because not knowing how to pray is no excuse when God has given so much information on how to pray. If we were free to pray only when we felt like it, it is very likely we would pray only when something extraordinary happens. Like being surrounded by guerrillas in a jungle village, or seeing number three engine on our jumbo jet burst into flames over the polar icecap, or having our baby daughter swallow an unknown quantity of mother's sleeping tablets. Now, by all means pray in these or similar situations! But prayer is much more than a last resort. Prayer is not something you do because circumstances have left you desperate; it is something you do because God told you to do it in order to develop a relationship with Him.

If we were free to pray when we had time and felt so inclined, it is unlikely we would ever have the time or the inclination. When did you last hear someone say as he looked at his watch during the interval at a ball game, "Good, I have a few minutes to spare, I must do some praying." Recently? No, if we pray only when we have time we will find that praying doesn't get done. And if we say we don't know how to pray and therefore don't bother, there is no way we will take the trouble to find out.

If we understand that prayer is a command, however, the whole picture changes. If we are told to do it by our Lord, then we discipline ourselves to pray when things are good and when things are bad. We do it when we have a pious feeling and when we don't. Prayer becomes a discipline when we are busy doing something and when we are busy doing nothing. Learning to do what we have been told to do becomes a top priority.

It may seem strange that the Lord found it necessary to command us to pray. It would seem that if we love the Lord and seek to know Him better, we would automatically pray and commands would not be necessary. Well, I find that even though I love the Lord and want to serve Him, there are so many things going on in my life, so many distractions in my world and so many responsibilities in my vocation, that however much I love

Him, I need a good, firm order from Him once in a while or I just don't get done the things that are easily missed. This is a bit like loving your wife. One would think that if a man loves his wife, he will automatically love to do everything he should. It will be impossible for him to fail because he loves her so much. But to think like that is to overlook the fact that he also loves his work, his football, his boat and his kids, and therefore, there are many clients for his attention and many demands on his time. Thus he faces the danger of taking his wife for granted and neglecting her, assuming all the time that she "knows that he loves her." He needs to discipline his time to do what needs to be done as an expression of his love for her. So, discipline is not the opposite of love, but rather it is often the evidence of love.

The third reason why we should pray is that Christ's example is unavoidable. To put it bluntly, if He needed to pray as much as He did, we certainly need to. I don't want to get into a whole study of our Lord's prayer life at this point, but I want to show you four important things.

Consideration No. 1—Christ's example. On numerous occasions the Lord disciplined Himself to turn aside from everything else and pray. If you find it difficult to do that, how do you think He felt? In Matthew 14:23, for example, we read that He went away quietly to pray, but first had to send the people away. Now, if there was one thing hard for the Lord to do, it was turning people away. He knew their needs as nobody else knew their needs. He had just fed five thousand families, and He knew the heartaches and the backaches in all of them. He had enough work in that crowd to keep Him busy for years, but He sent them away and went to prayer.

Then there was the time when He stayed up all night to pray, recorded for us in Luke 6:12. Missing a night's sleep is not easy, particularly when life is as full and busy as His life was at that time. Notice that just before His all-night prayer time He had a confrontation with the scribes and Pharisees which left them "filled with madness" and debating "what they might do to Him," and He was met immediately afterward by "great multitudes of people." The point is clear. Prayer with our Lord was a top priority. Nothing was allowed to encroach on that priority.

Consideration No. 2—Christ's expectation. That's a long title for a short section! The simple point of it is that when the Lord talked about the prayer experience of His disciples, He used the word when, not if: "When you pray . . ." In His thinking there were no "ifs" and "buts" about prayer—only "whens"! So it is clear He had a simple expectation that His followers would be people who among other things would pray regularly. This consideration must not be overlooked.

Consideration No. 3—Christ's explanation. One day the disciples came to the Lord and said, "Lord, teach us to pray" (Luke 11:1). So He did. First of all, He taught them what we call the Lord's Prayer. Most Christians know this prayer by heart. Some pray it every Sunday morning in their worship services; others know it well enough to recite on the rare occasions when they are called on to say a prayer. But this beautiful prayer is much more than a set piece used rather like the national anthem at sporting events. It is the Lord's answer to the disciples' request. They didn't say, "Teach us a prayer." They said, "Teach us to pray." There is a difference between praying and saying a prayer. You can teach a parrot a prayer, but I don't think you can teach it to pray!

The Lord's Prayer set to music is a favorite piece of blushing brides on their wedding day. Many times as I have officiated at weddings, the bride's sister or aunt has rendered Malotte's

"Lord's Prayer." It is among my favorite solos, even though I have heard it often. Yet, whenever I hear it sung at a wedding, I take five or ten minutes to explain to the congregation what it means—and invariably people come to me and say, "I have said that prayer for years, but I didn't know what I was saying." So I'll tell you what to do. Take every phrase of that prayer: Study it, think it through, ask the Lord to help you understand it and you will have learned an awful lot about prayer.

Before we move on to the next consideration, observe that after teaching them the actual prayer, the Lord told some parables about prayer. I learned in grade school that a parable is "an earthly story with a heavenly meaning." That's beautiful. One of my friends didn't quite understand. When asked to define a parable, he came up with the classic, "A parable is an earthy story with a heavy meaning." Never mind! Earthy or earthly, heavenly or heavy, parables are a magnificent means of getting the truth across. You should take a look at the parables the Lord used to describe what prayer is all about in answer to the request, "Teach us how to pray."

Consideration No. 4—Christ's exhortation. Exhortation is a nice Bible word. The dictionary says it means "the act of exhorting," which is a great help! But "to exhort" according to the dictionary is "to urge earnestly." Do you get the feeling that the Lord was in earnest when He was in the garden of Gethsemane? The place where He sweat blood? It was there He told His men to "watch and pray." Do you think He was "urging" them to pray when He told them they might "enter into temptation"? There is no doubt in my mind that the Lord was indeed earnestly urging them to pray because prayer was to be such a mighty necessity in their spiritual lives.

Thus we have some long answers to a short question. "Why

should I pray?" I hope the answers are stimulating enough and challenging enough to make you want to go further in the adventure of prayer.

4

What Should I Pray?

Many hang-ups about prayer must be sorted out before some people will get around to praying. A few persons get the idea from some of us preachers that God understands only "Olde fashionede Englyshe" and that unless they talk like King James and his merry men, God will not hear them. This naturally causes problems, because many people do get into tongue-twisting difficulties with *wilts* and *werts, thees* and *thous* and have heart attacks every time they even contemplate *lookedst* and *lettest.*

At the risk of offending friends who think antiquated terminology is the only valid expression of reverence, let me say definitely that prayer should be natural. So if thou naturally talkedst likest this, thou shouldest pray like this, but if thou dost not, thou dost not have to pray like this.

Nevertheless, the sense of reverence that all who really approach God in prayer must have demands standards of decorum and good taste that rule out silliness, looseness and glibness. If you talk to a person of some standing whom you deeply respect, you do so in a manner that expresses that respect.

To help you decide what to pray, I will spell out the word P.R.A.Y. this way:

P stands for Praise
R stands for Repentance
A stands for Asking
Y stands for Yourself

Praying includes praising God—worshiping Him and acknowledging Him and the wonders of His goodness and the greatness of His love. Immediately some of you will think you have a new angle on prayer in believing that prayer is the presentation of a celestial shopping list. But that is grossly underestimating prayer.

We must never forget that the greatest thing about being a human being, as opposed to a chimpanzee or a carrot, is, we can know God and "glorify Him." To glorify Him means to respond to Him in such a way that He is recognizable in our attitudes to Him. The way we think about Him, respond to Him, obey Him and thank Him is all part of glorifying Him. When we pray in praise, we do one of the most wonderful things humans can. We are glorifying Him in our attitudes and putting this into words. For me, one of the best ways is to read my Bible and, upon discovering something new about God or being reminded of something I'd forgotten about His character, to thank Him for being the kind of person He is and for doing the things He does. Let me give you an example. Before I began to write this chapter, I turned to my Bible and read Isaiah 48. In this chapter, many things are said about God. I didn't have time to make a list of them, because I was trying to get another chapter written! But I did bow my head and meditate on what it means that He is. After thinking about these things and thanking Him for them, I read verse 18: "Then had thy peace been as a river. . ." (KJV). Guess what hymn I started humming in praise! So I was able to praise the Lord at my keyboard!

Now, you will get material for your praise not only from the Scriptures, but also from another beautiful part of His revelation—nature. A quiet walk on a cool morning in the fresh beauty of a new day as yet unspoiled by nose-, eye- and ear-pollution will make your spirit rejoice. But remember, your praise should be directed to the One who made the day. You may find help in singing quietly,

> When morning gilds the skies,
> My heart awaking cries:
> May Jesus Christ be praised!

There is another area in which you should be stimulated to praise—answered prayer and blessings received. Saying "thank you" is common courtesy sometimes overlooked in our dealings with God. Do you remember that when the Lord healed ten lepers, 90 percent didn't say "thank you"? That is a sad statistic, and I fear it is repeated in our day too. Try being thankful regularly. A few Sundays ago, a ladies' group in our church sang, "Count your blessings, name them one by one." When they were through, I said, "OK, let's do what we were just told to do. Let's hear from you what blessings you have been counting lately and then we can be thankful together." The people were a little slow at first, but soon from every corner of the sanctuary came short, sharp "thank-yous" to the Lord for blessings received. All this is part of prayer. Praising is praying.

Second, prayer includes "repentance." When our children were small and we were trying to teach them to pray, we had three kinds of prayer: "Please prayers," "Thank you prayers" and "Sorry prayers." It will come as no surprise to you that we had no problem getting "Please prayers," slightly more of a problem with the "Thank you prayers," and the "Sorry prayers" were decidedly scarce. The children had the hardest time thinking of something for which to be sorry, When they eventually thought of it (usually with our help), saying "sorry" did not come easily. I'm afraid this is a problem which troubles many adults as well as kids. It really is difficult for us to admit we have done something wrong and even more difficult for us to say we are sorry about it. But whether it is difficult or not is beside the point. The Scriptures insist that we "confess our sins" and further promise that if we do, God will "forgive us our sins and cleanse us from all unrighteousness (1 John 1:9).

Perhaps a brief explanation here will be helpful. When a Christian comes to know the Lord, as we have seen, a new relationship develops. The Christian becomes a child of God, a servant of the Lord Jesus and the dwelling place of the Holy Spirit. Problems can develop in these relationship areas as they can (and do) in all relationships. For example, a Christian may behave in a way that is not suitable for a child of God. That behavior will not "unmake" him a child of God, but it will make the relationship between the child and the Father awkward.

When a Christian sins, his relationship remains intact, but his fellowship disintegrates. When the son of a prominent lawyer is indicted for smuggling heroin, the son does not become an "unson" because he has embarrassed his father. But feelings will be somewhat strained between them. The lawyer's son is still the lawyer's son even if the lawyer starts shouting about "disowning him." But they will not be living together like father and son.

When the Lord instructs His servant not to do something and he does it, the Lord is still the servant's Lord and the servant is still the Lord's servant. But nothing very much is happening. And when the Christian acts in a way contrary to the dictates of the Holy Spirit, the temple gets soiled. But it is still the temple!

This is where repentance and confession come into the picture. If a Christian goes on sinning, never admits it and never confesses, it is only a matter of time till he ceases to have any fellowship with the Lord and his effectiveness will be nil. But if he searches his own life carefully, exposes his sins and failings and is genuinely concerned about them, he will experience not only the joy of cleansing, but also the freshness of renewed fellowship.

Allow me to make some suggestions about confession and repentance. I have heard people pray at mealtimes and conclude with a phrase like "and forgive us our many sins." Now, this is good as far as it goes. It certainly shows that the person concerned is conscious of sin and is willing to deal with it and wants forgiveness and cleansing. But the prayer needs to be more specific. I find the words of the General Confession from *The Book of Common Prayer* very helpful:

> We have left undone those things which we ought to have done; And we have done those things which we ought not to have done; And there is no health in us. . . ."[2]

Notice three things: First, the failure to do expected things; second, the doing of forbidden things; third, the sense of personal unworthiness in the sight of God. These are necessary ingredients in prayer of this nature. But in our private and personal prayers we need to get more specific. Ask yourself, "What exactly did I do that I was told not to do? Did I sin with my eyes, my lips, my mind, my attitude? What exactly did I not do that the Lord expected me to do? Did I fail to love, to speak, to help, to give, to worship?" When you have some answers to questions like these, you are ready for confession and repentance. Of course, one of the by-products of repentance is that if you have to be repentant about the same thing often enough, you might get so embarrassed about it that it may produce the greatest incentive to turn from it and forsake it. Read Psalm 51 if you want an example of a man praying a prayer of repentance and confession.

Third, praying includes "asking." I realize I have put third what many people put first. And even I have found it necessary to keep a tight rein on my praying or I find myself doing the same thing. But remember that if praise is equivalent to "thank you," and repentance is equivalent to "sorry," then asking is equivalent to "please"—and to be interested only in please and forgetful about thank you and never sorry is to be extremely immature. So let's be thankful and sorry, and then perhaps we can start asking all over again.

There is no doubt that God wants us to ask Him for things. "Ask, and it shall be given you," Jesus said. "Seek, and ye shall find; knock, and it shall be opened unto you" (Matt. 7:7 KJV).

Ask
Seek
Knock

But for what kind of things can we ask? The best way for me to answer that question is to refer you again to the Lord's Prayer. Look at what the Lord taught us to ask for:

1. That God's name be honored and respected (6:9).
2. That God's kingdom be completed (6:10).
3. That God's will be implemented (6:10).

Note that your asking prayers should be motivated by these three great desires. This automatically rules out some praying like, "Lord, I want a Cadillac and You said 'ask and you shall receive,' so I'm going to extend my garage immediately in faith." That kind of prayer seems to have in mind the name and kingdom and will of the person praying more than that of the Lord! You don't need to get any hang-ups about this, trying to figure out whose will you have in mind at any one point, just as long as you don't think you can take off in any old direction and ask for anything that comes into your mind. If your heart is set on God's honor and will and kingdom, then His Spirit will lead you into the right prayer channels.

Now let's be more specific. The Lord's Prayer goes on to talk about your needing to ask about:

4. Physical needs—daily bread (6:11).
5. Social needs—forgiving and being forgiven (6:12).
6. Spiritual needs—temptation and deliverance (6:13).

Now, those three things cover vast areas of our lives and give us the green light to ask about things that are physical and social as well as spiritual.

But there is another important lesson to be learned from the Lord's Prayer. Read it to yourself and see how many times the words *I, me, my,* or *mine* occur.

Surprised to discover that none of them appears at all? Now, this is staggering when you think of the way we pray. The point is, when you ask in prayer you should be concerned with the name, kingdom and will of God as they relate to others. This is why I put "yourself" last in my outline on prayer.

What kind of people should we ask God to bless? I've just spent some time looking in my Bible for the answer to that question, and I've had a very interesting study. Abraham prayed for Abimelech, the man he had wronged (see Gen. 20:17). Moses prayed for the people who were under the judgment of God (see Num. 11:2). Samuel prayed for God's people who were in danger of making some bad mistakes (see 1 Sam. 8:6). Elisha prayed for a family in trouble (see 2 Kings 4:33). Hezekiah prayed for people in danger (see 19:15). Job prayed for his friends (see Job 42:10). Timothy prayed for monarchs and politicians (see 1

Tim. 2:1–2) . . . at least he was told to! Paul prayed for Timothy, who was a preacher and church leader (see 2 Tim. 1:3). Stephen prayed for his enemies (see Acts 7:59-60). And the Ephesians prayed for Paul, the missionary who was in prison (see Eph. 6:18–20).

This is not an exhaustive list—just a little exhausting! What a challenge it is to see all the kinds of people who need our prayers, and what a challenge it is to set about the task of praying for them!

Fourth, praying includes "yourself." Praying for yourself is not wrong. The Lord did it in the garden of Gethsemane, but remember that He said definitely He was not praying for His own will to be done, but God's. David prayed for himself on numerous occasions, and perhaps his most famous prayer is recorded in Psalm 51. But notice that he prayed for himself in order that sinners might be converted (13) and that God might be worshiped (19). I feel that we should have no difficulty praying for ourselves correctly if we remember that "Y" is the fourth letter in P.R.A.Y. The problem occurs only when we get "Y" up front. In fact, sometimes our praying is so out of order that we tend to do it this way:

Y for yourself
A for asking
R for repentance
P for praise

And you'll pardon me if I point out something: That is not praying, it's "yarping!"

5

When Should I Pray?

First, you should pray regularly. Daniel was so organized in his praying that even when he was forbidden to pray on pain of being thrown to the lions, he went ahead anyway and prayed three times daily. That was the way they did it in his day and, while it doesn't mean that you have to do it "morning, noon and night," it wouldn't be a bad idea! A friend of mine in England says every day should begin and end with prayer and a cup of English tea. Now, the tea is optional, but the prayer should be mandatory! I suggest that you plan a time of prayer into your regular schedule the way you plan eating and sleeping.

Your regular prayer should include regular attendance at church services where you can pray during the "pastoral prayer." In the church I pastor we lay heavy emphasis on the time of prayer in all our services. When the pastor prays in the service, that is not the time to think about your finances or whether you left the car's lights on, but you should pray along with him, letting his prayers become part of you.

For the same reasons, you should also form the habit of joining your fellow church members when they meet together to pray. It's a sad commentary of our attitude toward prayer that most church prayer meetings are poorly attended.

Then, you should pray regularly at your mealtimes. Even

when you eat out, you should bow your head in thanksgiving and witness—nothing ostentatious, but nothing to be ashamed of, either. Don't pretend to rub the nonexistent sleep out of your eyes, but don't spread your napkin on the floor beside your table and boom off a prayer for the benefit of the bemused diners near you. When my wife first bowed her head in thanksgiving in a restaurant, she opened her eyes to find an old woman looking anxiously at her and saying, "Here's an aspirin. Have you got a headache, luv?"

You should also try to have some regular prayer with your family if possible. They might not like the idea at first, but it's amazing how they can grow into it. Particularly the children. We have not done all we should with our kids in this matter, but what was done has been a delight. In fact, I enjoy praying with them as much as praying with anyone!

Doubtless there are other times when you can regularly pray, but I leave that to you. Do make sure that you pray regularly.

Second, you should pray spontaneously. Nehemiah did this beautifully. He had a job that wasn't the greatest—he was the king's cupbearer. That sounds fine until you read the job description. Among other things, he had to bring the king's wine to him and sample it—which to some may not sound all that bad, either. But the catch is this: people in those days had a nasty habit of putting poison into the king's goblet when they wanted him to take an early retirement; so Nehemiah was the "Royal Guinea Pig." Besides all this, he was not allowed to look unhappy in the king's presence. He had to enjoy his work!

One day Nehemiah received some bad news from home and naturally was upset. He forgot to put on his stage smile, and the king demanded why he was looking sad in his presence. That spelled trouble for Nehemiah, and he admitted to being "very much afraid"—but he took a deep breath and "prayed to the God of heaven" (Neh. 2:4). That doesn't mean he said to the king, "Every head bowed, every eye closed . . ." It means he flashed a very quick prayer to heaven in between heartbeats— something like "Help!"

This is what I call spontaneous praying. You will need to do it often when you are faced with danger or decision. The more you practice prayer, the more of a reflex action spontaneous prayer will become.

Third, you should pray continually. "Pray without ceasing" (1 Thess. 5:17) can raise some eyebrows. Those who think praying is done only in church will have to move into church permanently to pray without ceasing. Those who feel you must close your eyes and bend your knees to pray will become a terrible hazard when driving in that position on the freeway. Obviously this is not what the Bible has in mind.

Prayer is not only a definite act; it is also a continual attitude. The thought behind continual prayer is not that your life should be spent in the act of prayer, but that your spirit should live in an attitude of prayer. It is an attitude of humble thanksgiving, reverent awe, childlike dependence and expectant faith. It is an attitude that swiftly and easily, at the slightest sign of necessity ,slips into the act of prayer.

I know people who live in such a continual attitude of prayerfulness that sometimes I have noticed their conversation to be directed to me and without any warning redirected to the Lord.

This attitude is also of great help practically. Often I drive with the radio on to keep me awake. The information coming over the airwaves frequently stirs me to pray as I drive. As I run my morning mile, I run in an attitude of prayer. On the first lap

I pray for the family, on the second for the church and on the third for outside activities. The fourth lap? I pray, "Lord, give me breath for this unfinished task!"

6

How I Learned to Pray
More Effectively

This is a true story. A few years ago I was on a preaching tour in Africa. Late one night, after speaking in a school auditorium in Mwinilunga, Zambia, I was riding home with friends in their truck. A man had lit a fire on the side of the road, and in its light we could see he was asking for a lift. My friend stopped and the hitchhiker jumped onto the back of the truck with the baggage. A few miles further we stopped to let him off and he disappeared into the bush. When we arrived home, we discovered that my briefcase had disappeared with him. In it were my passport, airline tickets, lecture notes, the manuscript of a book I was writing, some shirts and overnight toiletries.

Nothing could be done that night, but early the next morning we went to the place where we had stopped to let our friend dismount. With the help of an African tracker we followed his trail to a small village. But all our questions fell on deaf ears. We persuaded one of the more helpful villagers to keep his ears open and let us know what he learned. Then we visited the local police and, after many inquiries, left the investigation in their hands.

Nothing happened for days. A rancher friend offered an ox

to the villagers who found and returned my briefcase; the people were hungry for beef, but we didn't hear a word. One morning a thought struck me with great force. We had tried a tracker, an eavesdropper, the police and an ox, but I had not tried prayer.

Chastened by my self-discovery, I went out to a quiet place overlooking the beautiful, rolling African bush and studied every reference to prayer I could find. Checking on the conditions of prayer, I came to the conclusion I could make some specific requests within those conditions and expect some answers. So I prayed specifically, asking for the things that were really necessary to the work I was doing to be returned. And nothing happened.

After about two weeks, I had to leave Mwinilunga for Kitwe and Ndola still minus passport, tickets, notes and manuscript. But still praying! Two more weeks passed, then the day before I was to leave the country, I received a phone call informing me some papers had been found in a ditch in the middle of the bush, but they were burned. As I was hundreds of rough and rugged miles from the charred papers, I wondered if I would ever see them. But some people drove overnight to bring them to me.

When I opened the parcel, I found my passport, my tickets, my notes and my manuscript. But no shirts or toilet gear. All I had asked for was there. Exactly! Nothing more and nothing less!

There was something else. I learned the briefcase had been emptied into the ditch; and the contents of interest to the thief had been taken, the rest left. Subsequently a bush fire came that way, but stopped at the place where the articles lay. They were all singed, but nothing was destroyed and not one letter on all the notes was indecipherable.

When I arrived home from Africa, a friend of mine stopped off in our home in England, having just completed a movie in Israel. He knew nothing of the details of my experience, but as he was leaving us to go to the airport, he thrust a package into my hand and said, "Here take these. I had to buy two of everything I was wearing in the movie in case we had to do a retake and my gear was at the cleaners." Inside the package were shirts—twice as many as I had lost in the bush thousands of miles away!

So I learned to pray, my friend had the joy of sharing, the African Christians saw a demonstration of God's answering prayer and one little man is running around the bush clad in shirts four sizes too big, smelling beautifully of Old Spice after shave.

7

How to Grow in Prayer

Praying on Your Own

This is a list I have drawn up for my own use. You may develop one more suitable for your purposes. If not, use this one!

1. Set aside a regular time for prayer.
2. Find a quiet place—bedroom, boiler room or boardroom!
3. Spend a few minutes in praise. Your Bible study should lead you into this.
4. Deal with matters of repentance. Ask yourself: (a)What did I do that I should not have done? (b)What did I fail to do that I ought to have done? Be specific.
5. Then start asking. Consider the Lord's Prayer for details. A prayer list of people for whom you wish to pray may be helpful. In your notebook or diary make a list of the people for whom you will pray each day. You may like to work out a system of praying for different groups on different days. For example:

Sunday pray for Saints—church members, the preacher, deacons, elders.

Monday pray for Missionaries—get a list from your missions board.

Tuesday pray for Teachers—Sunday school, public school, private school.

Wednesday pray for Workmates and Neighbors (bosses as well!).

Thursday pray for Troubled People—sick, divorced, starving, imprisoned.

Friday pray for Family and Friends—in-laws and outlaws.

Saturday pray for Seekers—those who don't know the Lord.

6. Conclude with some prayer for yourself. Deal with your own fears, hopes, desires and weaknesses.

Praying with Your Children

1. Don't expect them to be as pious as you. Remember what you were like at their age.
2. If you pray at mealtimes, don't expect them to pray fervently with the smell of rapidly cooling hamburgers in their nostrils.
3. If you do it at bedtime, don't get too excited about the length of their prayers.
4. Teach them the "Please," "Thank you" and "Sorry" approach.
5. Give them information about others for whom they can pray.
   A bulletin board in the den with missionaries' pictures, details of famine areas or other data is helpful.
6. Encourage them to be honest and natural, and do it yourself!
7. Don't go on at great length yourself. This will discourage their participation.
8. If they say something genuinely funny, laugh.

Praying in the Church

1. When the opportunity comes, don't duck it.
2. Remember: your objective is to speak to God, not to impress the congregation.
3. Don't use the prayer time to spill gossip or score a point.
4. Keep it short at first. A sentence qualifies as a prayer.
5. If you want to pray but think you'll dry up in the middle, write your prayer on a piece of paper. You can keep one eye open and one eye closed. You could say it is the "watch and pray" method.

Getting More People to Pray

1. Don't conclude a social time in your home without prayer.
2. Ask someone else to be a prayer partner with you. If you can't meet, pray together over the phone.
3. Develop a prayer chain. In our city there is a chain of women who pass along prayer needs to each other by telephone. In a matter of minutes, dozens of them can be mobilized into prayer. This can also be done via e-mail.
4. Inquire whether there are other Christians who would like to pray together in your school or workplace.
5. If there is insufficient interest in praying in your church, get people together in a different format.
6. Remember that someone has to get something started. If you are waiting for somebody else, they may be waiting for you!

Further Study on the Subject of Prayer

Get out your Bible and do a study on the following questions:

1. What are the conditions of prayer?
(a) John 14:13—It must be in the name of Christ.
(b) 1 John 5:14-15
(c) Jude 1:20; Romans 8:16, 26
(d) James 1:5-7
(e) Colossians 4:2

Think through each of these answers. You will need to pray about them!

2. What are some hindrances to prayer?
(a) 1 John 3:22—Disobeying and displeasing God.
(b) 1 Peter 3:6-7
(c) Matthew 5:23-24
(d) James 4:2-3
(e) Psalm 66:18

Further Reading about Prayer

A Passion for Prayer by Tom Ellif
Prayer: Expanded Edition by O. Hallesby
The Practice of Prayer by G. Campbell Morgan
The Power of Prayer by R.A. Torrey
Power Through Prayer by E.M. Bounds

The Bible . . . an excellent book on the subject!

Part III

REACHING OUT IN WITNESS

8

What Is Witnessing?

Just mention the word witnessing and some people run for their Bibles and booklets while others run for cover! It is strange, but the whole business of witnessing really gets to people in the Christian community. This is understandable in a way, because if "witnessing" is not adequately understood, it can indeed be scary.

A friend of mine tells a magnificent story of his first attempts at "witnessing." He was punched in the nose by a small boy and bitten on the leg by a large dog in no time at all! Needless to say, his enthusiasm ebbed as his blood flowed!

The word is used in various ways in the Scriptures. Leviticus 5:1 states that if a person is put under oath to be a witness and he does not testify truthfully, he will be held responsible. Obviously, this kind of witnessing has to do with courts of law where people are required to explain what they have seen and heard. Genesis 31 tells the story of those two rascals Laban and Jacob, who had spent years sharpening their wits on each other. Eventually they came to some agreement and built a big heap of stones as a "witness" to their agreement. In this sense, the word means to give visible evidence of an invisible experience.

Now, in the New Testament there is an interesting fact you should know about the word witness. The Greek word for "witness" is *martus*, and you don't have to know much Greek or English to see the connection between *martus* and martyr. In fact, in the gory days of the early church, to be a witness was almost a guarantee you would become a martyr.

If we put these three ideas together, we see that a witness is someone who by explanation and demonstration gives audible and visible evidence of what he has seen and heard without being deterred by the consequences of his action. That's my definition for what it's worth! If we can accept that definition, I think we can add one more thing and be ready to proceed. Christians have a particular subject in mind when they think of sharing their experiences and their convictions. It is their knowledge of Christ, from both the theoretical and practical points of view. So a Christian witness is someone who, in a variety of ways, communicates the truth as it is to be found in Christ.

I have labored over that definition because I find that many people have seen or experienced only one method of witnessing—and sometimes they have had a bad experience and decided never to witness again. I'm glad my friend who got beaten and bitten did not take this attitude, because he is now one of the most effective missionaries I know in the Spanish-speaking world. He discovered that some approaches to giving "audible and visible evidence" were not his line at all. But he didn't quit; he found other ways.

You may have tried going from door to door with *The Four Spiritual Laws* and loved it, but your partner curled up and died every time you rang a doorbell. You were praying, "Lord, give me the words to speak," and she was praying, "Lord, I hope they're not at home."

Or you and your husband may have been to a retreat at a conference center. You had a great time sharing with the people you stayed with and when it was your turn to "give your testimony" in the Sunday morning service, you took off and preached up a storm. But your husband couldn't wait to get home. When his turn came, he stood before the people, opened and shut his mouth like a goldfish with indigestion and sat down covered with confusion.

We can see that one method of witnessing may appeal to one person and other methods will appeal to other people. We must not lock people into any one system of doing it, nor must we allow people to overlook the necessity of their having an effective approach to witnessing.

But why is it important that Christians witness? Why can't the preachers get on with it while the other folks work to pay them for doing it?

First, Christ insisted that we should witness. In His famous last words, spoken on the Mount of Olives immediately before He ascended to heaven, the Lord Jesus said, "You will be my witnesses. . . ." (Acts 1:8). He said many other things at that point which help us to grasp the "how" and the "where" of what He had in mind, but right now let's concentrate on His bold statement, "You will be my witnesses." It is important to notice that the Lord did not say, "Wouldn't it be lovely if we could share a little of what we have learned with those who haven't had a chance to learn?" And He didn't say, "Hands up all those who feel like having a little witness!" No. His approach was straight and to the point. "You will be my witnesses."

The disciples got the message. It was unavoidable, and it should not be overlooked today. The point is not whether you will or will not be a witness. The point is that if you are a Christian, you are a witness and the only options open to you are whether to be "good, bad, or indifferent."

Once a woman is married, she doesn't decide whether or not to be a wife. She rejected that option the moment she took her vows. Her only remaining options are whether she will be a good wife or whether she won't!

It must be admitted that the Lord was talking to His select group of disciples when He gave these instructions. Thus some people today believe these words were applicable only to those who heard them. But always remember that the Lord taught His original disciples so they might teach others until the whole world knew about Him. Therefore, these things do apply to us today. He still says, "You will be my witnesses."

Second, Christ did a lot of it Himself. The variety of our Lord's ministry is one of its most beautiful characteristics. Whatever else He was accused of, He was never accused of being in a rut. Sometimes He spoke to crowds about "lilies" and "ravens," and other times He gave them "spectaculars" like feeding thousands with a few loaves and fishes. He was at home preaching in a formal synagogue or from a fishing boat. Professors or prostitutes, He spoke to them all.

It is this fact of Jesus' willingness and eagerness to speak to the individual as well as to the crowds that is important to us in this study. Sometime you should read through the Gospels, looking for the personal conversations that the Lord Jesus had with individuals. It will be of great help to realize how much personal evangelism He did.

The Lord is many things to His people and not least our example. The point is obvious. If He is our example, perhaps His witnessing is to be an example, too. Not all pulpit preachers are skilled personal witnesses. Not everyone who can hold a crowd in the hollow of his hand can take a child in the crook of his arm. But Jesus could and did, and in the busyness of my own ministry I try not to forget His example in this respect. Neither do I easily forget the words of the old preacher (Spurgeon, I think) who said, "Preaching is like throwing a bucket of water at a row of bottles. Some of the water goes in some of the bottles. But personal witnessing is like taking the bottles one at a time and carefully filling them." You may not be called or equipped (or inclined) to be a preacher, but you are to witness as Jesus did.

Third, God ordained that we should be witnesses. If you are not familiar with 2 Corinthians 5, take a few minutes to read it. Notice particularly two things Paul said in verse 18: First, he (and others) had been reconciled to God and second, they had been given a ministry of reconciliation. Then, before the shock of that had time to settle, he said in verse 19 that God was doing the reconciling and had committed to "us" the "message of reconciliation."

If a preacher says the same thing twice in the space of ten seconds, it can mean

(a) he forgot what he was saying;

(b) he has more time left than material;

(c) he is trying to emphasize something.

When the Bible does the same thing it means

(a) it is trying to emphasize something!

The emphasis should not be difficult to understand. If you have been reconciled to God, you have been given a ministry of reconciliation. On the one hand, you were given reconciliation and, on the other, a ministry. Many people do not figure that God works this way. But He does. He gives blessings in order to make the blessed become the means of blessing. What He puts in He expects to pop out. With God, input leads to output.

You can't be reconciled to God without being recruited! This is the way He ordained it. That being the case, the world must be teeming with people in the reconciliation business. But the problem is many of them either don't know they are in it or know but wish they didn't.

Fourth, the world needs us to be witnesses. I didn't say the world wants us to be witnesses, but it certainly needs us! Take a look at the last verse of James' epistle. It's a beauty. "Let him know that he who turns a sinner from the error of his way shall save a soul from death and cover a multitude of sins." (NKJV) Three things are mentioned in this verse that a human being can do for another person.

1. He can convert him from the error of his way. This means some people are living their lives in error. Some know they are, but many don't. Think of it for a minute: There are people with whom you rub shoulders every day, and they are heading in the wrong direction with every step they take. They are building their lives on a false foundation; they are living lifestyles based on a false philosophy; they are filling their hearts with false hope.

They are in error. They are in danger of arriving at the wrong destination and not knowing it till they get there. It is possible that the whole of their lives will be devoted to meaningless causes while important issues are never considered. This is frightening.

But—and it's a big but—you can change all that. Through an effective witness to Christ, you can lead that person from error to truth.

2. He can save his soul from death. If you jump into the river and pull someone out, you'll be a hero. Yet you will have saved someone from death only to have him die later. Don't mis-

understand me! If you get the chance, do it. But if you realize that saving someone physically is little more than postponing the inevitable, how about considering saving somebody's soul? If you want to be a real hero, do something more than postpone the inevitable—change his whole eternal destiny.

To be dead to God in the depths of the soul is to be devoid of the knowledge of God, to be alienated from the life of God and cut off from the kingdom of God. Spiritual deadness is at the root of much of our marital, political, social and even international ills.

But you can be the means of changing that through the witness of Christ to those who are spiritually dead. You can lead a person from death to life.

3. He can cover the multitude of his sins. People with marital problems have told me they have found it more difficult to forget than to forgive. With the best will in the world, they have tried to forgive and forget, but it has not always been possible. "Time is a great healer," as they say, and gradually the wounds heal in most cases. And it takes a considerable amount of concentration on the past for a person with a failing memory to remember all the things he is supposed to forget. They just tend to drip away in the end, or become so confused with other things that there is more fantasy than reality left.

Now, think of something else. God doesn't have a failing memory. He doesn't overlook sin and He is eternal, so that what we call the past is the present to Him, and what hasn't happened yet is in the now with Him. If this is confusing, it is also sobering, because it means the considerable mind of God is fully aware of all that has gone by in our lives. And all that has gone past includes an awful lot of sin—"a multitude of sins."

This is serious beyond description because people are responsible beings who must stand before God and give an answer for their sins. No evasion, no postponement, no tricky defense lawyer. Just man and God and a multitude of sins. But one thing we need to remember: God can "put away sin," "hide it in the depths of the sea," "remove it as far as the east is from the west" and "remember it no more" —all because Christ's sacrifice for sin is applicable to all who come to Him in repentance and faith.

You can tell people about that by being a witness to Christ's saving death and resurrection. You can tell people there is forgiveness through the grace of God. You can cover a multitude of sins.

One thing is obvious, but needs to be made more obvious. When it says (and when I repeated) that "he" does the converting and the saving and the hiding, the Bible means God does all this and the man is the means of it being done.

Can you think of a greater need in our world than the need for the saving, restoring, enriching message of Christ to be given to more and more people? Can you think of anything more exciting than to be caught up in meeting that need? I can't!

There are many other answers to the question "Why is it important that Christians witness?" But I believe the four I have mentioned are sufficient.

9

What Must I Do to Be a Witness?

It is possible to understand all the reasons why Christians should witness, believe them thoroughly, get all convicted and convinced—and never do a thing about it, in much the same way that you can watch a documentary film about famine in sub-Saharan Africa, hear the appeal for funds, switch off the TV and go to the fridge for a pizza. At first glance this would appear to be nothing more than callous indifference. But I believe further scrutiny would reveal that this is not altogether true. There is a sense of hopelessness and helplessness in the attitude of both the famine-watchers and the silent witnesses. They really feel that the situation is out of control and whatever little they can do would make no difference whatsoever; so they turn away and try to forget what they know.

I am convinced, however, that we must not only show the need but also take the people by the hand and lead them so they can really discover that there is hope and that they can help. In this way, they can be motivated not to despair, but to involvement.

As for witnessing, I am sure that if more people were shown exactly what to do, they would lose their sense of hopelessness and helplessness and get moving. So let me explain what you need to do.

You will need to get some concern. That's great, isn't it? You didn't need someone to tell you that. You know you should be concerned, and the thing that concerns you is that you're not concerned! Nevertheless, there is no way of avoiding this point, for if you are not concerned about the spiritual condition of people, you will do nothing to alter their condition. The problem, as I see it, is that many people feel guilty because of their lack of concern, but don't know how to get some! Let's attack this problem before we go further.

1. There are spiritual reasons for a lack of concern. When the Holy Spirit is really working in your life, He motivates in very special ways. He gives you a love for things you used to dislike, and a distaste for things you used to enjoy immensely. He also begins to deal with inbred selfishness and produce an outlook that recognizes the conditions of those around you. This transforming work of the Holy Spirit in regard to your desires and dislikes inevitably leads into an experience that makes you see as He sees and eventually love as He loves.

But you can stop Him from doing this work in your life. You can "grieve" Him and "quench" Him. When the fire of the Holy Spirit begins to burn in your heart to such an extent that you see people as He does and decide to reach them as He does, you may find a reaction in your own heart. If you aren't too careful, you may allow your reaction to His working to become stronger than His working. Then you're in trouble, for you are hindering the gracious working of the Holy Spirit, quenching His motivation and grieving Him. You will have concerns that are yours and not His, and in all probability, your concerns will have to do with things other than reaching people with the good news.

What can you do about this kind of situation? First, recognize it when it happens, admit it to yourself, and then confess it to the Lord. Tell Him, "Lord, I'm just being selfish at present. I know from Your promptings in my heart that I should be thinking about the needs of Mrs. Finkelschnitzel who is in the hospital, frightened and discouraged; I know You are bringing her to my mind, and I know I could take her a word of comfort from the Scriptures. But to do that I would have to miss my hair appointment and . . . ."

That is being honest, but it isn't enough. So decide whether you are going to say, ". . . and Lord, I won't quench your Spirit; and I won't grieve you, I'll cancel the appointment. I'll go and see her for your sake! And I'll wear my wig."

2. There are theological reasons for a lack of concern. Anyone who has done any Bible study at all is aware that such words as hell, condemned, perish and wrath are found in rather large quantities. This emphasis is unavoidable, but that does not mean we find it to be totally acceptable. The fact of the matter is that many "Bible-believing Christians" don't really believe what the Bible says when what it says is challenging and sobering.

Herein lies the problem: If people who are believers don't really believe what they profess to believe, there is a great need for them to reevaluate their theological position and have the courage to abide by its implications. That means, if you believe there is a hell and people are perishing and under the wrath of God, you must let their spiritual condition move you into concern that will move you into action. If, on the other hand, you do not accept the reality of these things, then feel perfectly free to be unconcerned about people's spiritual well-being.

A journalist with whom I was talking in Switzerland recently summed it up beautifully. He said, "There are some who believe that people without Christ are lost, and others who believe that people without Christ are not lost. Those who believe that there are lost people have no alternative but to be concerned about the lostness of these people; but those who do not believe that people are lost can spend their time talking about issues other than the spiritual needs of mankind." He was right. Yet the problem we face is that many who believe people are lost want to behave like people who don't believe people are lost. This is a luxury the Bible does not offer to them.

So, get your theology cleared up at this point. Are people lost or aren't they? Is there a hell or isn't there a hell? Do people face the wrath of God or don't they? If your answers are in the affirmative, then let your theology get into your bloodstream and take it to its conclusion. After that the concern will come.

Gen. William Booth, founder of the Salvation Army, could never be accused of mincing words or doing things halfheartedly. He believed if he could hold each of his young Salvation Army officers over hell for a few minutes, he would never have any trouble keeping them motivated about being witnesses to Christ.

3. There are practical reasons for lack of concern. Feeling a concern for witnessing can mean that you will have to stand up and be counted, and this can bring some degree of abuse. Years ago I was praying with one of my children at bedtime, and I asked him if he had any problems we should pray about. He couldn't think of any, even though I could think of a number! Rather unwisely, I pressed the point and asked, "Don't you have any problems at school?"

"No," he replied quite firmly.

"Don't the kids give you a hard time because you're a Christian?"

Again the answer was "No."

Thinking back to my own traumatic school days, I said, "But kids always give you a hard time if you let them know you're a Christian."

His reply was frank beyond belief: "All the more reason you don't let them know!" And quite happily, he turned over to sleep.

With the refreshing candor of the very young, he had put into words the practical reasons why many Christians don't witness. They don't want to take the consequences. In all fairness to my son, who may even read this book one day, I must explain that he now sees things differently and has been used by God in numerous lives he's interacted with.

Another practical problem is that some people are willing, but they feel they are not able. Perhaps many people would witness if they knew how. Others believe they don't know enough, and so if they open their mouths they will put their feet in. These feelings are frankly understandable, but always remember that God does not expect you to share what you don't know. He does expect you to share what you do know. If you are primarily concerned with how you will come out of any witnessing activity, your concern for your image outweighs your concern for those who really need the Lord. That is obviously all wrong.

Thus, if you are lacking in concern for people, let me suggest the following things:

1. Find out if any selfish motivations are controlling your actions so that the Holy Spirit can't control them. Recognize this as wrong, confess it and ask the Holy Spirit to give you His

concern for those who need the Lord.

2. Check your theology, particularly the parts relating to man's condition before God. Then find out if your behavior is consistent with your belief. If it isn't, ask God to help you have the courage to be consistent.

3. Make a list of all the hang-ups you have about witnessing. Pray about each one and begin to see them in the light of what God has told you to do.

4. Continue to do these things, because if you don't, you will find other concerns taking the place of this concern.

You will need to make some contacts. Scripture uses numerous pictures to illustrate the activity of witnesses. At different times we are called fishermen, ambassadors, reapers, watchmen. These occupations have little in common. It is unlikely you will ever mistake an ambassador for a night watchman, or think that a man wading to his middle in a river is cutting oats. But they do have one important thing in common: Fishermen have to make contact with fish, reapers have to go where the oats are, watchmen have to be right where the action is and ambassadors have to present themselves at the court of the nation to which they are sent. They all have to make contact.

The whole business of making contact is difficult for many people. So difficult, in fact, that they refuse to do it. Then they have to defend their position by putting the blame on the other party. Some Christians seem to think people do not find Christ because they don't go to church. But I think the real reason is because the church doesn't go to them. Fishermen don't sit at home grumbling because the fish aren't knocking at the door asking to be caught. Reapers don't account for their lack of harvest by blaming the oats for not jumping into the barn. And the U.S. ambassador to England certainly doesn't sit in his apartment and say, "If the Queen wants me to be an ambassador to her country, she'd better come to Washington and get me." The responsibility to make contact rests on the witness or the fisherman or whatever you want to call him.

It is a rare person who has no contacts. Even lonely old ladies see the mailman occasionally. Most people have hundreds of people with whom they rub shoulders. Start thinking about all those people you know. Has it ever occurred to you that you could reasonably expect to be a witness to them? It might help you to make a list of all the people with whom you have any kind of contact. Then start to pray for them and ask God to give you a chance to talk to them sometime.

The people on the top of your list will probably be relatives, friends and workmates—the people whom you see on a regular basis. You obviously have a person-to-person contact with them as husband or son or boss or tennis partner or business competitor, and it may be that you are known only in these capacities. But it is necessary that you be known also as a Christian in your contact with them. This will require some words on your part, but perhaps the old adage "actions speak louder than words" is more important in this kind of contact because of its enduring nature.

You can't talk to these people all the time about Christ without them either locking you up or divorcing you, unless you get laryngitis first. It is necessary for you to establish standards of behavior in your relationships with these people that begin to express your commitment to Christ. This behavior will be the result of your reading the Word of God and obeying it. It will be the product of the Holy Spirit's ministry in your life changing you from what you were, more and more into what you should be. This kind of behavior speaks volumes.

In my new members' class at church recently I heard the story of a whole family who came to an experience of Christ because of the changed life of one of their sons in junior high school. His behavior had so completely turned around that his family couldn't help but see the difference. He had made contact. Once you feel you are making some kind of consistent impression upon the people close to you, one of two things will happen. Either they will come to you asking questions, or you will go to them asking them questions. You will need lots of wisdom and tact, but plenty is available and you should plan on using it. When people begin to recognize you for what you are, they will know to come to you when they need what you have to offer.

On numerous occasions in my business life, I remember that men came to me when they had spiritual needs simply because a contact had been made which did not threaten them; when they wanted to go further, it was really quite easy for them. You should aim to build up this kind of long-term contact. But some of them never will come to you. When you think the time is ripe, you should go to them and ask them if you might share something with them that is very important to you. Because of the respect they have for you as a result of your relationship with them, it is unlikely they will refuse to listen to you.

Don't be in too big a hurry with the people whom you see every day. If you get after them too quickly and too crudely, you may well close their ears and their minds for a long time. I know young wives who have come to Christ and have immediately lowered the boom on their unsuspecting husbands. Often the husbands, when they have climbed out from under the boom, are less than enthusiastic about their wives-cum-evangelists. This is understandable. They figure that if they are so bad as to need all this evangelizing, why were their wives so foolish as to get hitched to someone so bad! Or if she isn't foolish, she must be as bad. Either way, she hardly qualifies in his eyes as a budding Billy Graham! A little tact and patience go a long way!

The basic requirements for building up a long-term contact with people whom you wish to lead to Christ are:

(a) Care
Make sure you exercise great care in living consistently and attractively before them.

(b) Dare
You will need more courage to witness consistently over a long period to someone close to you than you will need to speak to someone you don't know and who doesn't know you.

(c) Share
If you want to make a lasting impression, share yourself with the person. Get involved in his interests, get your shoulder under his burdens and be genuinely glad when he has a success.

(d) Prayer
Don't discount the effectiveness of prayer in the preparation of people's hearts for the good news.

One of the most common difficulties in this regard is caused by a person's losing his friends when he makes a commitment to Christ. Sometimes this is because the friendship of the non-Christian is so superficial that it cannot rejoice in the newfound happiness of the Christian. But often it is caused by the new Christian's losing contact with the old friend, either because of fresh involvements (more meetings than movies), or a feeling that continuing friendship with people who are not Christians is contrary to the biblical teaching on "separation." Never confuse "separation" with "isolation." Jesus showed the difference between having no part in the sinner's sin (separation) and having no part in the sinner's life (isolation). Always separated, He was never isolated. The Hater of Sins was the Friend of Sinners.

So make sure you don't lose your old friends because of your actions, but be prepared to lose some of them because they reject your Lord and your lifestyle. When my wife came to Christ as an undergraduate at Cambridge, most of her college friends rejected her, but two stuck with her. Their friendship never wavered, and years later both of them found the Savior.

Similarly, when one partner in a marriage finds Christ and the other doesn't, an obvious problem develops. Particularly if the ingredients listed above are not mixed into the marriage. It is not uncommon for a young wife to tell me, "Since I became a Christian six months ago, I have had nothing but trouble with my husband. Before I made my commitment everything was fine, but now we argue and go our separate ways and I'm worried." And so she should be.

I tell these young women, "You are not the person you were six months ago, and for that you can thank God. But you are not the person whom your husband married either. That means he is married now to someone he didn't date and someone he doesn't know and someone he didn't marry. He is living with a different girl. See it from his point of view. No wonder he's sore and confused and bitter. You altered everything. That means the onus of responsibility rests on you. He hasn't changed. You have changed.

So far we have been talking about "long-term contacts" that continue week after week, in which you see the person concerned virtually every day. Now we need to talk about the "short-term contacts."

Many opportunities of presenting Christ come your way

daily in casual contacts. Just yesterday, I heard a former business-man tell how he never started to serve a customer without first telling the customer about Christ. The cynics among you may be tempted to say, "That's why he's a 'former businessman.'" And I would find myself sharing your sentiments except that I know he was a successful businessman who retired at the age of sixty-two to do missionary work among Muslims in North Africa.

This, though an unusual case, points out that even in the everyday life of the business world there are numerous contacts in which Christ can be shared. But before you go overboard, remember you are being paid to sell mutual funds, not eternal security!

Traveling presents many chances to share Christ with fellow travelers, unless you are traveling in England where people tend to bury themselves behind their newspapers, emerging only to view solemnly and silently any new arrivals before returning to matters of prime importance like the football scores! Yet, even in that kind of situation people will talk if you are patient and courteous.

One important thing about these casual contacts is this: in God's eyes they are not casual. There is a great principle of God involved in all this. God says that if people really seek after Him with all their hearts, they will find Him. But most people need someone to help them find God. That means three people are involved: The God who is supervising the operation, the seeker who may or may not know he is seeking and the person who will be God's means of seeing that the seeker finds. If you can think of the world as being full of seekers and God as knowing every one of them and organizing circumstances so these seekers find helpers, I think you will see where you fit into a divine plan. If you will only tell the Lord you are on call all the time and are eagerly awaiting the opportunity to help seekers find God, there is no doubt God will send seekers your way.

This is really exciting. Whenever you start a day by reminding the Lord to call on you if there is anyone in your vicinity who needs help—you expect someone to show up once in a while. Every person you meet may be that person. This keeps you alert like nothing else I know!

Reuben A. Torrey in his book *How to Work for Christ* meticulously provided details about all kinds of approaches to every conceivable type of Christian outreach. He must have been an exhilarating character with a great drive to reach people wherever possible. He explains in his book how to make contact with people on a streetcar: You should always try to sit where there are two empty seats; then you sit in the seat next to the aisle so the people can't get out when you start to talk to them! He added that you should make the seat next to you look as inviting as possible! That sounds magnificent, and when I see him in glory I'm going to ask him how to make a streetcar seat look inviting!

Despite his quaintness, Torrey was saying, "Think about the person who will sit next to you whenever you sit down, and look for a chance to talk to him about the Lord."

As a pastor, I often visit people in the hospital, but I have found that few of them have private rooms. This means there is usually at least one other person in the room. I always make a point of talking to them, too. Sometimes as I walk along the corridors of the hospital, I look through the open doors of the wards and see lonely people lying there gazing at the ceiling. Bad as it may be looking at me, I think it must be worse looking at the ceiling, so I often go in and talk to them. They are nearly always very grateful. It's simply another way to make contact!

The key to the matter is to believe that there are seekers all around you and that the Lord will reach them through helpers. Go around with a sense of anticipation that you are going to get in touch with your share of these people. And remember, always be interested in people. Look at them, enjoy them, be alert to them, listen to them and give them the feeling they matter to you.

My wife once exclaimed, as we were working with some way-out kids who looked like a disaster area, "Aren't kids gorgeous!" We often say the same thing now, except that we've amended the statement to "Aren't people gorgeous!" The response depends on how you look at them; but if you start seeing them as individuals who hurt and love and whom Christ loved to the point of death, you will get hooked on people and love to make contact for Christ's sake.

You will need to make conversation. If you want to get the message across to people, sooner or later you must get into conversation with them. I realize that some people are more gifted than others when it comes to talking; but unless there is an impediment of some kind, everyone has the ability to say what he thinks with some degree of skill. Settle for the fact that while you may not be an orator or an intellectual, you still know how to explain a recipe to your friends or what happened in the ballgame last Sunday. Once you do this, you can be sure you can engage people in conversation that will witness to Jesus Christ. There is no basic difference in talking to people about Irish stew, American football, or the Lord, except for the subject matter. In all cases you have to know some facts, gain people's attention, assume they are interested, use words to explain your understanding and answer questions that might arise.

So there is no sound reason why people should be reticent about having a conversation about the Lord Jesus, even if they know little. Thousands of cooks who share recipes are not cordon bleu cooks. And how many men talk football who could never be mistaken for Brett Favre or Pelé. You don't have to be the angel Gabriel to witness. So let's look more closely at this matter of conversation.

Talking to people about their eternal destiny is indescribably solemn. Never forget it. Those who talk about spiritual realities must be aware they are meddling with souls. This is enough to freeze the most fluent tongues. But there is another consideration. Over and over again the Scriptures assure us that the Lord is in our witnessing. "Open your mouth wide, and I will fill it" (Ps. 81:10), "Behold, I have put my words in your mouth" (Jer. 1:9). "I will be with your mouth and teach you what you shall speak" (Exod. 4:12). "It is not you who speak, but the Spirit of your Father speaking through you" (Matt. 10:20).

An understanding of these two things will deliver you from being blasé and careless on the one hand and uptight and reticent on the other. You can't be glib when you understand the solemnity of it all, but you can't be uptight when you grasp the promises concerning God's working.

There are a few points you should learn if you wish to have effective conversations about the Lord.

1. Learn how to participate in ordinary conversations. Many people think Christians are bores because they have only one topic of conversation. Many times these critics have valid grounds for their criticism. Make sure no one can say this about you. Be alert to what is going on around you and take time to formulate opinions about what is going on. When the conversation veers in the direction of these subjects, be ready to share your opinions. This way you will earn the right to be heard when you want to direct the conversation toward Christ.

Another point not to be overlooked is that your Christian convictions will usually make a definite contribution to the conversation whatever the subject may be. If you begin to think this way, not only will you have many opportunities to witness, but you will probably raise the standard of conversation immeasurably.

In addition to the many contemporary issues of the day, there are dozens of perennial issues like sports, sex, death and marriage. All these topics are worth discussing—but I caution you: Don't get into a discussion merely on which team will win the Super Bowl. See if you can elevate the discussion by introducing something like, "Why is it that football fans will sit in subzero weather for three hours to watch a football game, but will walk off the job if their offices aren't heated to sixty-eight degrees?" That may sound like a silly issue to raise, but I assure you, it isn't. The answer has something to do with commitment and that is a more beneficial topic than who will win the Super Bowl.

If someone should mention abortion, try to defuse the potentially explosive subject by directing the discussion into an examination of the nature of life, the source of life and the meaning of life. Not only will this aid any discussion on abortion (you can't argue convincingly about destroying life if you haven't defined what you are destroying!), but it will lead people into serious consideration of great subjects that relate to their own humanity.

2. Learn how to start conversations about spiritual issues. Don't assume that witnessing opportunities will always be served up to you on a plate. Often they have to be initiated. Remember how the Lord started the conversation with the woman at the well recorded in John 4:7: He asked the woman for a drink. She was startled because it was not the "done thing" for a man

to start a conversation with a woman in those days. Times have changed! As a result of His initiative, however, the whole city of Sychar was reached.

Philip took similar action when he approached the eunuch driving back to Ethiopia. He asked the man, who was reading a scroll he had bought in Jerusalem, "Do you understand what you're reading?" Blunt and to the point and wonderfully effective—because the man said, "How can I, unless someone guides me?" Read Acts 8 if you can't remember the sequel to the story.

Nathan the prophet started something too. He told King David a heartrending story about a rich man who stole the only lamb of a poor neighbor, killed it and served it to a guest. David was irate about it all, but was stopped cold when Nathan said, "You are the man!" Quite a conversation! Particularly when you bear in mind that it was initiated by the prophet and he was addressing a king. Read the whole story in 2 Samuel 12.

These incidents illustrate three ways of starting a conversation. In the first one, a general remark is made with the intention of leading into a fuller conversation. This can be done easily. "Hello, how are you today?" spoken to someone lying in a hospital bed can elicit the response, "Well, I can't grumble." which is usually a prelude to a recounting of ills and woes. Pious platitudes may help a little, but words of comfort—and particularly words of wisdom concerning the whole subject of suffering—will be most helpful and you may find yourself in a most profitable conversation.

I entered a hospital room by mistake one day. Two women were there and when I saw I had been directed to the wrong room, I apologized and was about to leave. But one of the women said, "Don't go. Stay and talk to us."

"All right," I replied, "let's talk about Jesus."

They were astonished but recovered quickly, and I stayed for most of the afternoon explaining the Lord to two hungry hearts. One of the women wrote to me later and said, "The talk we had was the highlight of my week and explained many things I didn't understand."

A second effective way to start a conversation is to ask the person, "What do you do?" He may answer, "Do you mean what is my job?" Then you reply, "Well, that's part of it. I'm just interested in people, and I like to know what interests them." They usually tell you, then ask what you do. That's where it gets easy, because you can always tell them about your job and your hobbies and no doubt your interest in the work of the Lord.

At one stage of my business career, I had the privilege of entertaining bank personnel at dinner on the bank's expense account. Many of those we entertained were more interested in liquid dinners than more substantial fare. I found this an awful bore, but it was also a beautiful opportunity to share with them. When they ordered their liquid meal, I ordered bitter lemon or tomato juice or something equally innocuous. It nearly always threw my colleagues for a loop. "You're kidding," they would say, enjoying the joke. But I would point out I wasn't joking: I had some definite convictions about booze. "There's nothing wrong in a drink or two" was the inevitable response, with which I agreed. But I led the discussion into "But where do you draw the line?" and then I would explain where I drew the line and my reasons (which were that I worked with young people and felt that my example in this area was important).

The whole point of the conversation soon became a discussion of the need for adequate spiritual leadership for the young by parents and youth workers and not a fight about "What's wrong with a drink or two?" Often I have seen the drinks forgotten in the ensuing conversation, with businessmen searching their hearts as they consider their spiritual responsibility as examples to the young people around them.

The third illustration I have given is a classic example of "setting somebody up." Nathan did it beautifully. Poor old David, by his violent reaction to Nathan's story, condemned himself before he realized he had been set up! I must say, great care should be exercised if you do this kind of thing. Sometimes when I see people reading the paper, I say to them, "More bad news?" "Yes," they reply, "what else is there?" Well, I think you know the answer to that, don't you? Or the conversation may go along the lines, "It's unbelievable what's going on, isn't it?" "Right! Things seem to go from bad to worse." "I sometimes wonder what on earth the world is coming to . . ." When someone says that, tell them what the world is coming to!

Of course, there are more structured ways of doing this, such as going up to someone and saying, "Have you heard of the 'Four Spiritual Laws'?" If they say no, then you know what to say and you get into your presentation. If they say, "Yes, I have— 999 times and if anyone else mentions them to me, I'll separate them from their breath!"—then you must adapt!

3. Learn how to have a discussion without getting into a fight. This is more easily said than done if you have my kind of temperament. I love arguments, but I have given them up for the sake of the kingdom. My problem was that I could usually make someone look foolish even if I couldn't beat them in the argument. So it became a battle of wits, and having been gifted with quick wits, quick tongue and quick humor—if not with much knowledge—I could effectually hide my ignorance behind various smoke screens.

But I didn't lead people into the blessing of God that way. I learned to admit that I didn't know something, if that was the case. This made me appear honest to the person with whom I was speaking, and they sensed that my primary interest was truth, not conquest.

Some time ago, I participated in a radio program in which people called in with their questions and comments. It went on for about three hours, so we had a wide variety of topics and experiences. Some people came on the air to bluster their ignorance, others to make a point, some to get even and a few to ask questions. One young man spoke with great erudition about Egyptology, and when he had explained what he wanted to say, he said, "Now, how does your statement fit into what I have just said?"

I replied, "I haven't the remotest idea, because I have no knowledge of what you obviously know very well. So thank you for sharing what you have studied so thoroughly, and I want you to know that I have learned a lot from what you said."

Months later, I was officiating at a wedding, and the best man came to me afterward and said, "I know you, but you don't know me. I called you on a radio show one night and talked about Egyptology." I knew him immediately! He went on, "I was so impressed when you didn't evade the issue and you admitted your ignorance that I listened to the whole show although I had initially called just to embarrass you. I like honest people."

Be fair to people, be honest with people and you won't start an argument. If the other person does not respond and obviously wants a fight, say, "Do you want an argument?" and if he says yes, tell him to go somewhere else because you are interested in discovering the truth and sharing it rather than just having fun at someone else's expense.

4. Learn to handle questions adequately. Please note that I didn't say learn all the answers. Personally, I have a problem with people who know all the answers, because frankly, I don't think God has given us all the answers. Anyway, there are some questions that don't merit answers. No doubt you have come across the wise guy who wants you to be his straight man. He asks questions he does not want answered; in fact, if you did answer him, he would be mortified.

You need to learn how to deal with his kind of question. Moreover, you need to try to sense the attitude of the questioner before you attempt to answer his question. For example, "Where did Cain get his wife from?" can be asked in different ways and should, accordingly, be answered in different ways. When Mr. Wise Guy asks me that question as if he thought of it, I sometimes say, "I'm sorry, I don't know. I wasn't invited to the wedding." Or, "I would tell you if I were Abel." (Note the pun!) However, this can be a genuine difficulty with some people who believe that Adam and Eve started it all and had two sons and from them the whole human race developed. Obviously they will wonder about Cain's wife. The answer, shocking as it may seem, is, "Presumably he married his sister because there wasn't anybody else."

Or, you may find a militant atheist asking you, "Why does your God allow war?" Your answer would have to deal with the whole subject of morality if there is to be any adequate handling of his question. On the other hand, someone who has suffered terribly in a war may ask the same question, not with belligerence, but with bewilderment. You will have to deal with this person much more gently and much less intellectually than the first person. The former needs a rational answer, the latter needs a compassionate one.

The sooner you come to terms with the fact that you do not know all the answers—and probably never will—the sooner you will feel at ease with people. If you don't know, say so. If you aren't sure, say, "I think the answer lies in this area, but quite honestly, I'm not sure." And if you have a certain ambivalence, admit it. Once I had to give the answer, "Well, some say this and others say this and some people say this, but honestly, I'm not too impressed with any of these answers, and I would be more inclined to think this."

A word of caution is needed. I am not suggesting that you should be less than dogmatic when the Scripture is clear and plain. But neither should you feel it necessary to be dogmatic when Scripture isn't.

There we are. Try some of these approaches and have some good conversations as God gives you the opportunities.

10

The Need
to Bring Matters
to a Conclusion

Fishermen rarely get excited about influencing fish. It's landing fish that is important to them! Farmers think in terms of harvest; watchmen give warning in order that people may be saved. So it is with witnesses! They think in terms of bringing their witness to a conclusion. Their desire is to bring people to commitment and regeneration. But many witnesses have real problems at this point, for they seem unable to bring things to a satisfactory conclusion.

Not everyone is going to become a believer, of course. Not everyone to whom we witness will be ready to make a commitment at the time we happen to speak to them. But by the law of

averages, if we keep sharing, sooner or later someone will come
our way who wants to finalize something! When that happens,
many witnesses turn chicken. Let's look at this phenomenon:
The fisherman who doesn't want to land the fish he has hooked,
or the farmer who doesn't harvest the grain he has sown, or the
watchman who doesn't expect people to accept his warnings!

Fear is one of the chief causes. The consequences of a Christian conversion are frightening to some people, and often the
person witnessing is more aware of this than the person about to
make a commitment. For example, the things that will happen
in the marriage of a new Christian may be extremely traumatic
when he begins to reject the lifestyle which he and his wife had
adopted for years. Or, the businessman about to make a decision
is not altogether clear what is going to happen in the executive
suite when he begins to apply biblical ethics to a corrupt business enterprise—particularly if it will cost the whole company
considerable money. Or, the kid who jumped bail after being
busted for drugs has to return and face the authorities as soon
as he becomes a Christian, and that means a year or two in the
slammer for him.

Witnesses who understand these ramifications are sometimes
tempted to pull back at the last minute rather than be responsible for what is going to happen to the person who is converted.
If this sounds unthinkable, let me tell you frankly that I have
been involved in situations similar to these; I have been tempted
not to follow through for fear of the consequences of conversion,
both for the new believer and sometimes for myself.

Doubts may be a cause. Self-doubt can be paralyzing at a
time of spiritual conflict. Suddenly you're confronted with a person who wants to be led to Christ. This person is really going to
step out of darkness into light, from the power of Satan to God,

from death to life! The recording angel's pen is poised, the angelic choir director's baton is raised, heaven waits for the repentant sinner's prayer—and you can't go through with it! You just don't feel worthy to be involved in something so momentous! You fear you are so inexperienced that you'll foul it up; so you back off and say, "Well, don't rush things, why not go away and think about it, talk to your parole officer (or wife!) and maybe we can have another chat sometime."

Perhaps you doubt the sincerity of the person to whom you're talking. You doubt whether he knows enough to make an intelligent decision. I've often been assailed by this kind of doubt when dealing with people. Some years ago my wife and I were the guests of the Billy Graham team in their crusade at Shea Stadium in New York City. When the invitation was given on a particular night, hundreds of people streamed onto the playing surface of the stadium and it was obvious there were more inquirers than counselors. So we went down to help. I walked up to a young man who was standing alone and said to him, "Why did you come forward?"

He replied, "Because I've seen it on TV and I've always wanted to do it."

"In what way do you feel you have been helped by doing this?"

"Oh," he replied, "this is what the world needs. We need to stand together. We need to settle our differences."

I wondered how much this young man understood of what was going on, so I asked, "What part of Dr. Graham's message helped you most?"

"None of it," he replied. "I wasn't here to listen to anyone speak, I came to stand with the people." It was perfectly clear to me that he knew nothing of the significance of the invitation and had no thought of Christ.

I was tempted to go and talk to someone else, but something about this young man's honesty attracted me; I stayed and explained the gospel to him. At first, he didn't appear to be interested, but then he asked a few questions and suddenly said, "Okay, how do I make this commitment?" As far as I knew, he had had no contact with the message of Christ before our conversation. Yet after about twenty minutes of explanation, he was asking to be led to Christ. You'll understand that I had some real doubts about the situation, but in response to his request we prayed together. After taking a note of his name and address, we parted. I wrote to him the next day, never expecting to hear a word from him, but a long letter came to me in just a few days.

In no time at all, this young man became identified with a group of believers, engaging in Christian service. His regular letters, while increasingly becoming less frequent, were always full of the joy of the Lord—and needless to say, full of thanksgiving for the time we had together in Shea Stadium!

Ignorance is also a cause. Not knowing what to do is probably the biggest reason we don't do most things. This is certainly the case when it comes to leading people to Christ. One approach I have found helpful personally is to ask three direct questions to the person to whom I have been explaining the gospel.

1. "Do you need Christ?" The purpose of this question is to ascertain whether the person has understood the point of his need and the fact that only Christ can meet the need. It is an appeal to the mind, and it is important, because if a person does not understand why he or she needs Christ, there can be little hope of a valid experience of regeneration. When you are reasonably satisfied that the person is reasonably clear about this and answers, "Yes, I do need Christ," then you should go on to the

second question.

2. "Do you want Christ?" You must never assume that a person who knows he needs Christ will automatically want Him. Needs and wants don't always go together. Some people need to have their teeth fixed, but they don't want to go to the dentist! Many persons intellectually agree with the fact of their need and the ability of Christ to meet it, but they have no desire to go to Him. Therefore, you must address this question to their emotions to discern whether there is a real longing for Christ.

You should never hide anything about the claims of Christ from a potential disciple. There must be no "small print" in the contract you get people to sign with Christ. Jesus was very emphatic about this when He insisted that people "count the cost" before making a decision. I like to be clearly satisfied in my own mind that people understand what it is Christ requires of them; after I have explained it, I often say, "Now that you understand what you're getting into, do you still want Christ?" If they say, "Yes, I understand fully and I still want Him," I ask the third question.

3. "Are you willing to receive Christ?" Having addressed the mind ("Do you need Christ?") and the emotions ("Do you want Christ?"), you must challenge the will. This is crucial, because knowledge about Christ and the emotional appeal of Christ of themselves cannot produce regeneration. The will must submit to the claims of Christ and express its acceptance of the promises of Christ before the person concerned receives Him.

It's rather like getting married. Before arriving at the altar, the couple have expressed some degree of understanding of what marriage is about. Their presence also shows their desire to get married. But only when they have answered the "Will you . . ." in the affirmative do they become united in marriage.

Nevertheless, some believers insist belief alone is necessary for salvation, and accordingly, they resist any suggestion of conditions needing to be fulfilled. They would not agree with my statement concerning a willingness to "submit to the claims of Christ."

The illustration of marriage may be helpful in this respect also. No one can expect to enter into a healthy marriage relationship without a willingness to accept the responsibilities of that relationship. Yet no young man on the day of his wedding really knows what he is saying when he talks about "love and cherish..., in sickness and in health, for better for worse, for richer for poorer . . . , till death us do part." This does not mean he is being insincere; it simply means he is willing to accept all the ramifications of being married even though he has no way of knowing what these ramifications will be. But he is ready to find out and willing to make the commitment to respond to them as he does.

In the same way, a person making a commitment to Christ cannot possibly know all that is involved in acknowledging Him as Lord. But he must express his willingness to submit to the Lord he knows, on the understanding that he will get to know Him a whole lot more as the years roll by. The more he knows, the more he will submit to what he knows.

Suppose you are confronted by someone who has convinced you he needs Christ, he wants Christ and he is willing to receive Christ. What then? Let's return once again to the marriage service. Rarely do I meet young people who are confident enough to be able to recite their marriage vows on the big day. Usually I have to help them as I officiate at the wedding. So they repeat the vows after me. This does not mean their vows are unreal; it simply means that at the moment of stress they need some prompting. When you are dealing with someone in the stress situation of regeneration, you will probably need to help him pray. Usually I ask the person concerned if he would like to pray after me, and most times he says he would like that very much.

The prayer should be short and to the point. Though I have no set way of doing it, I believe a prayer of this kind should always include admission of need, a statement of repentance, an expression of trust and dependence and a note of thanksgiving. It may be like this: "Thank You for loving me enough to die for me, Lord Jesus. I acknowledge that I have sinned, and I ask You please to forgive me. I also know I'm not strong enough to live as I ought to, but I understand that You are prepared to come into my life by Your Spirit to give me new strength. Please do this right away. I ask You to be my Lord and my Savior. Thank You for hearing this prayer. Thank You for answering it, and thank You for all that You will do in me, for me and with me in the future. Amen."

11

The Need to Be
Willing to Continue

At this point you may be thinking, "Good! That does it! That's how to bring things to a conclusion and that finishes what needs to be done." Strange as it seems, there is something after the conclusion. (It is a bit like my sermons which have been known to continue long after their conclusion!) After the conclusion we must be involved in continuation. Weddings take only a few minutes, but marriages are intended to last a lifetime. Receiving Christ doesn't take long once all the preparatory work has been done; but rearing a new Christian is a long and sometimes painful procedure. Unfortunately, many people committed to witnessing about Christ are not so enthusiastic about leading the convert into a mature experience of Him. But they must understand the importance of this; otherwise they may be guilty of deserting someone at the time of his greatest need.

Immediately after praying a prayer of commitment, many people are desperately unsure of themselves. Truly, some people may experience a great sense of relief, and others will feel as if a great burden has rolled away. Some may even laugh, and others will probably cry. But most will look at you with a "now what?" expression on their faces. You must have some "now what" information for them.

Help them to be clear about what has happened. People sometimes expect a blinding flash, a radiant glow, or some other kind of experience or feeling to follow hard on the heels of their prayer. Explain to them that feelings can be fickle, and if they expect to experience unusual phenomena or pleasant feelings all the time, they will be disappointed. If Christian experience were dependent on these things, then headaches, backaches and stomachaches would destroy it—unless, of course, adequate medication was available. And then the Christian experience would tend to depend on drugs!

Help the convert to see that Christian experience is based on the promises of Christ; these, when acted upon by the believer, become reality. Christ always keeps His promises. When He said, "If anyone hears My voice and opens the door, I will come in," (Rev. 3:20) He meant it. Anyone hearing and opening can be certain Christ has done exactly what He said He would do.

Encourage them to thank the Lord for what He has done. You may meet a person who says, "I received Christ hundreds of times." Such a person needs instruction. Tell him, "You can't go on receiving Christ, because if you've got Him, you've got Him. It is important for you to understand this so you can get on with something else. If you spend all your time receiving the One you have received, you'll never discover who the One is whom you have received."

I usually illustrate this by offering a dollar to the person whom I am counseling. "I'll give you this if you would like it," I say (hastening to add this is only an illustration, so he won't be embarrassed and so I will get my dollar back!). When he says,

"Please may I have it?" I give it to him and he replies, "Thank you very much." I point out that he said "Please" before he received and "Thank you" afterward. When he has received, he does not persist in saying, "Please may I have it," for the simple reason he already possesses it. He says, "Thank you." Then I make sure he understands that once he has received Christ he should not continue to ask Him to come into his life, but should say the courteous thing: "Thank you for coming into my life." I encourage the consulter to begin to thank the Lord that He has done what He promised. He should get into the habit of being thankful. I tell him to say "thank you" when he wakes up, before eating a meal, as the last thing at night and whenever he thinks of Christ. This kind of thankfulness can be a great encouragement to all kinds of Christians.

Give them the opportunity to tell someone what they have done. "If you confess with your mouth that Jesus is Lord and believe in your heart that God raised him from the dead, you will be saved" (Rom. 10:9) is a vitally important verse. It stresses (along with many similar verses) the absolute necessity of believers saying what they believe or confessing Christ. I believe modern evangelism has produced some ingenious methods that have helped thousands of people come to Christ; but I am concerned that some of these methods ask people to do things other than confess with their mouths. Raising hands or walking down aisles or even waving hymn sheets no doubt has a real value in helping people crystalize their thinking into action; but they leave something to be desired if they become substitutes for people's speaking about Christ and sharing their experience of Him.

New believers should be helped to say what they have experienced as soon as possible. Whenever a new believer begins to speak, it becomes relatively easy to know to what depth he has experienced Christ. It is important that you know this, because if you do not understand how much he understands, it will be extremely difficult for you to help him further. So encourage him to express what has happened and make sure you are listening carefully. The other reason is that all believers are expected to be witnesses; the sooner they get started, the better it will be for all concerned. Thus, introduce the new believer to someone who is sympathetic and give him a chance to talk about the Lord. I have never known anyone who refused to do this, and I have seen dozens of people begin their ministries minutes after coming to the Lord simply because it was expected of them. After they have "broken the ice," tell them to keep going and they will find great certainty building up in their own hearts as they begin to thank the Lord and begin to share what they know of Him.

Give them literature they can take away to read. I don't mean you should give them a copy of Berkhof's *Systematic Theology* or Calvin's *Institutes*. This will not be necessary! First, find a little booklet that explains in simple language what has happened, so that when they get away from your influence and the impact of the great encounter begins to wane a little, they will have something to turn to. There are many booklets of this nature available. You should get well stocked at a Christian bookstore; then, when the opportunity comes, you will be adequately prepared.

Arrange to have further contact. Explain that new Christians need lots of help in their experience of Christ and that you would like to provide part of the help. This takes time and effort on your part, but it is vital for the well-being of the new believer. If possible, try to do some or all of the following:

(a) Provide or recommend good reading materials and check to see that the believer is reading and understanding them.

(b) Introduce them to things Christians do. Take them to

church with you or take them along when you go to visit some-body in the hospital or get them to help you in whatever Christian service you perform. You should not just tell these people what to do, but make opportunities to do it with them.

(c) Pray with them, study the Scriptures with them and encourage them in this way to grow in their knowledge of the Lord.

(d) Take an interest in what interests them—be it music or sports or collecting antiques. And if you aren't interested, try getting interested! It will be good for you and show the new believer that Christians are people and not merely animated Bible machines.

The overall objective in any kind of ministry—including witnessing—is to bring people to maturity. Though maturity is obviously relative, we must stay with people until they have had many opportunities to grow.

Part IV

DISCOVERING GOD:
A Personal Bible Study

Discovering God

This personal Bible study is designed to encourage you to dig into the Word of God for yourself. Satan, your relentless enemy, will do everything he can to keep you from finishing even the first lesson. Bible study is work, but it's a work of joy. Paul the apostle charged a young Christian, Timothy, to "study to show thyself approved unto God, a workman that needeth not to be ashamed, rightly dividing the word of truth" (2 Tim. 2:15 KJV).

This study has been arranged to help you to "rightly divide" the Word of God as to who God is and what He does. From your study you will gain important knowledge that will cause you to mature and be equipped for living and serving (see 3:16-17).

DIG IN

1. Take your study and note the subject given in the major heading.
2. Read each question and look up every reference.
3. The reference will give answers to each question. Write the answer in the space provided.
4. Underline the references neatly in your Bible for further use.

5. Learn by heart the verses suggested in each study. This will enable you to have a few key verses on each subject readily available in your mind for the Holy Spirit's use day by day.

6. Allow God to speak personally to you through this study of His Word.

PRACTICAL SUGGESTIONS

1. If possible, obtain a file or notebook in which to keep your completed studies.

2. Use a dictionary and look up words you do not understand.

Study No. 1

WHAT IS THE BIBLE?

- Men have been looking for God since time began.
- God wants to be found.
- You can find Him through the Bible, the Word of God.

1. *How does the Bible describe itself?*
        (1) Luke 8:11
                <u>God's Word is like a seed</u>
        (2) Psalm 119:105
                A. _____
                B. _____
        (3) Jeremiah 23:29
                A. _____
                B. _____
        (4) Ephesians 6:17 _____
        (5) Psalm 19:9–10
                A. _____
                B. _____
        (6) 1 Peter 2:2 _____

2. *From your answers above, what do you think the Bible should do in your life?*
        (1) <u>Seed—Bring forth fruit (character) in my life</u>
        (2) _____
        (3) _____
        (4) _____
        (5) _____
        (6) _____

3. *With what subjects does the Bible deal?*
        (1) Philippians 2:16 Life — it is the Word of Life__

(2) Ephesians 1:13 _____

(3) Acts 13:26_____

(4) 2 Corinthians 5:19_____

(5) Hebrews 5:13_____

4. *What did Jesus say about the Word of God?*

(1) Matthew 4:4 We live by the Word of God_____

(2) Matthew 22:29_____

5. *What ought I to do with the Word of God?*

(1) Isaiah 34:16 Seek it out and read it_____

(2) 2 Timothy 2:15_____

(3) Psalm 1:2_____

(4) Acts 17:11_____

(5) Psalm 119:140_____

(6) Luke 24:45_____

(7) Psalm 119:9_____

(8) Psalm 119:11_____

(9) Acts 11:16_____

(10) Hebrews 4:2_____

(11) James 1:22_____

(12) John 8:31_____

6. *In what ways is the Bible of value to me?*

(1) 2 Timothy 3:15_____

(2) John 20:31

     A._____

     B._____

(3) 2 Timothy 3:16-17, It is profitable for

     A._____

     B._____

     C._____

     D._____

    E._____

    F._____

(4) Psalm 119:9_____

(5) Psalm 119:11_____

(6) Psalm 119:130

    A._____

    B._____

(7) Romans 15:4_____

(8) 1 John 5:13_____

(9) 1 Peter 2:2_____

7. *How is it possible to abuse the Word of God?*

  (1) Mark 7:13_____

  (2) 2 Corinthians 2:17_____

  (3) 2 Corinthians 4:2_____

  (4) Titus 2:5_____

  (5) 1 Peter 2:8_____

  (6) Revelation 22:18-19

    A._____

    B._____

8. *Learn the following verses and references by heart.*

  James 1:22; John 20:31; Psalm 119:105

Underline neatly in your Bible all the verses you have studied.

Study No. 2

WHO IS GOD?

- Men have invented many gods.
- But there is only one God.
- He created the universe and man.

1. *This one God consists of three persons (sometimes called the Trinity).*

> What are the names of the members of the Trinity?
> Matthew 28:19
> A. <u>Father</u>
> B. _____
> C. _____

2. *The members of the trinity work together.*

In the beginning God the Father _____ the heavens and the earth (Gen. 1:1). The Spirit of God _____ (Gen. 1:2). All things were made _____ God's Son and _____ Him (Col. 1:16). Jesus was _____ by John the Baptist, and the Spirit of God _____ upon Him, and God the Father said, "_____ _____" (Mark 1:9–11).

> (1) *What was the relationship between Father and Son?*
> A. Galatians 4:4 <u>The Father sent the Son</u>
> B. John 3:16 _____
> C. John 5:20 _____
> D. John 8:28 _____
> E. John 8:54 _____
> F. John 10:15 _____
> G. John 10:18 _____
> H. John 11.42 _____
> I. John 6:57 _____
> J. John 11:41 _____
> K. John 17:4
>> (a) _____
>> (b) _____
> L. Luke 2:49 _____

(2) *What was the relationship between the Father and the Holy Spirit?*

        A. Acts 1:4–5 _____

        B. John 14:26 _____

        C. 1 John 4:13 _____

(3) *What was the relationship between the Son and the Holy Spirit?*

        A. Luke 1:35 _____

        B. Luke 4:1 _____

        C. Luke 4:18 _____

        D. Hebrews 9:14 _____

        E. John 14:26 _____

        F. John 15:26 _____

        G. John 16:14 _____

3. *What is the attitude of the Trinity to the world?*

    (1) Father—John 3:16 _____

    (2) Son—1 Tim. 1:15 _____

    (3) Spirit—John 16:8 _____

4. *What is the attitude of the world to the Trinity?*

    (1) Father—John 17:25_____

    (2) Son—John 15:18_____

    (3) Spirit—John 14:17_____

5. *What should my attitude be?*

    (1) To Father—John 4:23; Deut. 6:5_____

    (2) To Son—John 20:31; Col. 2:6

        A. _____

        B. _____

    (3) To Spirit—Eph. 5:18; Gal. 5:16 _____

6. *What should I not do?*

(1) Father—Deut. 8:11_____
(2) Son—2 Tim. 1:8_____
(3) Spirit—Eph. 4:30; 1 Thess. 5:19_____

7. *What should my experience be?*
    2 Corinthians 13:14
    (1) Father_____
    (2) Son_____
    (3) Spirit_____

8. *Memorize the following verses:*
        John 3:16;   Colossians 2:6;   1 Timothy 1:15

Study No. 3

WHAT IS GOD LIKE?
*   God wants us to know He exists.
*   But He also wants us to know Him personally.
*   We need to know what He is like.

1. *What are the characteristics of God?*
    (1) His attributes
        A. Leviticus 19:2 He is holy_____
        B. John 17:25 _____
        C. 1 John 4:8 _____
        D. 1 Corinthians 1:9 _____
        E. Genesis 21:33 _____
        F. Genesis 17:1 _____
        G. Deuteronomy 4:31_____
        H. Joshua 3:10 _____
        I. Nehemiah 1:5
                (a) _____
                (b) _____

    J. Jonah 4:2 _____

    K. Romans 15:5_____

    L. Romans 15:13_____

    M. Romans 15:33_____

    N. 2 Corinthians 1:3_____

(2) His autobiography

Exodus 34:6—He says He is:

    A. _____

    B._____

    C._____

    D._____

    E._____

(3) His faithfulness

    A. 1 John 1:9_____

    B. 1 Corinthians 10:13_____

    C. Lamentations 3:22-23_____

    D. Hebrews 10:23 _____

    E. 1 Thessalonians 5:24_____

    F. 2 Thessalonians 3:3_____

(4) His ability

    A. Hebrews 7:25_____

    B. 2 Timothy 1:12_____

    C. Jude 1:24

        (a)_____

        (b)_____

    D.Romans 14:4_____

    E. Ephesians 3:20_____

    F. Romans 4:21_____

    G. Acts 20:32

        (a)_____

        (b)_____

      H. Hebrews 11:19 _____

      I. 2 Corinthians 9:8 _____

2. *What about God and man?*

    (1) Genesis 1:27_____

    (2) Genesis 6:5_____

    (3) Psalm 26:2_____

    (4) Romans 1:18_____

    (5) Romans 2:16_____

    (6) Romans 5:8_____

    (7) 2 Peter 3:9

        A._____

        B._____

        C._____ _____

    (8) 1 Timothy 2:4

        A._____

        B._____

    (9) Acts 17:30_____

    (10) John 14:23

        A._____

        B._____

3. *What will God be to me personally?*

    (1) Psalm 23:1_____

    (2) Psalm 27:1_____

    (3) Psalm 28:7_____

    (4) Psalm 94:22

        A._____

        B._____

    (5) Psalm 18:2

        A._____

        B._____

        C._____

D._____

E._____

F._____

G._____

H._____

4. *What should I be to Him?*

   (1) 2 Timothy 3:17_____

   (2) John 1:12_____

   (3) Romans 8:16-17

      A._____

      B._____

   (4) Titus 1:1_____

5. *What must my attitude be to Him?*

   (1) Psalm 116:1_____

   (2) Psalm 37:3_____

   (3) Psalm 37:4_____

   (4) Psalm 37:5_____

   (5) Psalm 37:7

      A._____

      B._____

6. *Memorize the following verses:*

   Romans 5:8;   2 Corinthians 9:8;   1 Corinthians 10:13

Study No. 4

IS JESUS CHRIST GOD?

- God sent Jesus into the world.
- He came to show God in language we understand.
- But how can we know Jesus is God?

1. *Because of the prophecies He fulfilled*
   (1) In His birth
      A. The Old Testament (Gen. 3:15) said He would be . .
.   The New Testament (Gal. 4:4) said He was . . .
      <u>born of a woman</u>

      B. Genesis 18:18 said He would be . . .
      Luke 3:33–34 said He was . . .

      C. Numbers 24:17 said He would be . . .
      Luke 3:33–34 said He was . . .

      D. Genesis 49:10 said He would be . . .
      Luke 3:33–34 said He was . . .

      E. Micah 5:2 said He would be . . .
      Matthew 2:1 said He was . . .

      F. Isaiah 7:14 said He would be . . .
      Luke 1:26–35 said He was . . .

   (2) In His life
      A. The Old Testament (Isa. 9:1–2) said He would . . .
      The New Testament (Matt. 4:12–16) said He was . . .

      B. Isaiah 61:1-2 said He would be . . .
      Luke 4:16–21 said He was . . .

      C. Psalm 69:9 said He would . . .
      John 2:14–17 said He was . . .

      D. Isaiah 35:4–6 said He would . . .

Matthew 9:27–35 said He was . . .

_____

(3) In His betrayal and trial
　　A. The Old Testament (Ps. 41:9) said He would . . .
　　The New Testament (Mark 14:10) said He was . . .

_____

　　B. Zechariah 11:12 said He would . . .
　　Matthew 26:15 said He was . . .

_____

　　C. Psalm 27:12 said He would . . .
　　Matthew 26:60–61 said He was . . .

_____

　　D. Isaiah 53:7 said He would . . .
　　Matthew 26:62-63 said He was . . .

_____

　　E. Isaiah 50:6 said He would . . .
　　Mark 14:65 said He was . . .

_____

(4) In His death
　　A. The Old Testament (Isa. 53:12) said He would . . .
　　The New Testament (Matt. 27:38) said He was . . .

_____

　　B. Psalm 22:6–8 said He would . . .
　　Matthew 27:39–40 said He was . . .

_____

　　C. Psalm 22:18 said He would . . .
　　Mark 15:24 said He was . . .

_____

　　D. Psalm 69:21 said He would . . .
　　Matthew 27:34 said He was . . .

_____

E. Psalm 34:20 said He would . . .
John 19:31–33 said He was . . .

_____

2. *Because of the claims He made*
   (1) Luke 22:69–70 _____
   (2) John 14:7–10 _____
   (3) John 8:58 (see Exod. 3:14) _____
   (4) Mark 14:61–62 _____
   (5) John 9:35–38 _____

3. *Because of the miracles He performed*
   (1) Matt. 4:23-24 _____
   (2) John 11:38–44 _____
   (3) John 6:9–14 _____
   (4) Mark 5:1–17_____

4. *Because of the attributes He displayed*
   (1) Omnipresence (He can be everywhere)
   Matt. 18:20; John 2:24–25
   (2) Omniscience (He knew everything)
   Mark 11:2–4; John 4:16–19
   (3) Omnipotence (He could do anything)
   Matt. 28:18; John 19:28

5. *Because of the testimonies He received from:*
   (1) Father—Matt. 17:5
   (2) Peter—Matt. 16:16
   (3) John—John 1:1
   (4) John the Baptist—John 1:34
   (5) Paul—Acts 9:19–20
   (6) Andrew—John 1:40–41
   (7) Nathanael—John 1:49
   (8) Samaritan woman—John 4:29

(9) Martha—John 11:27
(10) Centurion—Mark 15:39
 (11) Devils—Matt. 8:28, 29

6. *Because of His resurrection*
He was declared to be the Son of God by the _____
(Rom. 1:3–4)

7. *Memorize the following verses:*
John 10:28;   Matthew 17:5;   John 1:1

"But these are written so that you may believe that Jesus is the Christ, the Son of God, and that by believing you may have life in his name." (John 20:31).

Study No. 5

WHY DID CHRIST LIVE?
- God isn't a vague being.
- He is a living reality.
- The life of Christ shows us how real.

1. *Jesus Christ was both God and Man.*
  (1) What divine characteristics did He display?
      A. Divine power
         a. Matthew 8:26_____
         b. John 10:18_____
      B. Divine knowledge
         a. Matthew 17:27_____
         b. Luke 5:4–6_____
         c. John 6:64_____
         d. John 19:28_____
      C. Divine preparations

       a. Mark 8:31_____

       b. Luke 9:22_____

       c. John 7:33_____

(2) What did He reveal about God?

       A. 1 Timothy 3:16_____

       B. 1 John 4:9_____

       C. 1 John 2:11_____

       D. 1 John 1:2_____

       E. John 17:6_____

(3) What human characteristics did He display?

       A. Matthew 20:34_____

       B. Luke 2:40_____

       C. Luke 4:2_____

       D. Luke 8:23_____

       E. Luke 9:58_____

       F. John 4:6_____

(4) What human limitations did He have?

       A. John 8:28_____

       B. John 5:19_____

       C. John 5:30_____

(5) What was the principle of His life?

       A. John 14:10_____

       B. John 8:29_____

       C. John 5:30_____

(6) Why did He come into the world?

       A. 1 Timothy 1:15_____

       B. John 10:10_____

       C. John 18:37_____

       D. John 12:46_____

       E. Matthew 9:13_____

       F. Luke 19:10_____

       G. John 6:38_____

       H. Galatians 4:5

           (a)_____

           (b)_____

2. *What effect did His life have on*

      (1) The devil?—Matt. 4:1–11_____

          John 14:30_____

      (2) The disciples? —Luke 5:8_____

          Mark 6:51_____

      (3) The people? —Mark 5:42_____

          John 7:46_____

      (4) His enemies? —Luke 23:4_____

          John 7:1_____

3. *What is the value of His life?*

      (1) Shows me what God is like

          A. Colossians 1:15_____

          B. John 14:9_____

      (2) His sinlessness condemns my sinfulness

          A. 2 Corinthians 5:21_____

          B. Hebrews 4:15_____

          C. 1 Peter 2:22_____

          D. 1 John 3:5_____

      (3) Shows how God expects life to be lived

          A. John 6:57_____

      (4) His sinless life qualified Him to die for sinners

          A. Isaiah 53:6_____

          B. 1 Peter 1:15_____

4. *Memorize the following verses:*

      1 Timothy 1:15;   1 John 4:9;   1 Peter 3:18

Study No. 6

WHY DID CHRIST DIE?
- God didn't send Christ just to live.
- He sent Him to die.
- You need to understand the meaning of His death.

1. *What is the meaning of Christ's death?*

Romans 5:8—"While we were still sinners, Christ died for us."

    (1) Christ's death was violent

        A. What were His physical sufferings?

                John 19.1_____

                John 19:2_____

                Matthew 26:67_____

                Isaiah 50:6_____

                John 19:18 (see also 20:25)____

                Read Psalm 22:14–18.

        B. What were His mental sufferings?

                Luke 22:44_____

                Matthew 27:29_____

                Luke 23:35_____

                Luke 23:39_____

                Matthew 26:56_____

        C. What were His spiritual sufferings?

                2 Corinthians 5:21_____

                Isaiah 53.6_____

                Mark 15:34_____

                Isaiah 53:10_____

    (2) Christ's death was voluntary

        A. Hebrews 9:14_____

        B. John 10:17–18_____

    C. John 15:13_____

(3) Christ's death was vicarious (on behalf of others)
    For whom did Christ die?
    A. Hebrews 2:9_____
    B. Romans 5:6_____
    C. Romans 5:8_____
    D. 2 Corinthians 5:15_____
    E. Ephesians 5:25_____
    F. Galatians 2:20_____
    G. Romans 14:15_____

(4) Christ's death was victorious
    What did His death accomplish?
    A. Hebrews 9:26_____
    B. Revelation 1:5_____
    C. 1 Peter 3:18_____
    D. 2 Corinthians 5:21_____
    E. Galatians 1:4_____
    F. Ephesians 1:7
               (a)_____
               (b)_____
    G. Romans 5:10_____
    H. Hebrews 2:14_____
    I. 1 John 1:7_____

2. *What is sin?*
    Romans 14:23_____
    James 1:14–15_____

(1) How is sin committed?
    A. Proverbs 10:19_____
    B. Proverbs 14:21_____
    C. Proverbs 24:9_____
    D. James 4:17_____

    E. 1 John 3:4_____
  (2) Which people commit sin?
      A. Romans 3:23_____
      B. 1 Kings 8:46_____
      C. Ecclesiastes 7:20_____
  (3) Why do people commit sin?
      A. Psalm 51:5_____
      B. Romans 7:14_____
      C. Romans 7:20_____
      D. Mark 7:21–23_____
  (4) What are the results of sin?
      A. Romans 6:23_____
      (See also 1 Tim. 5:6; Rev. 3:1; 20:12–14.)
      B. Psalm 66:18_____
      C. Isaiah 59:2_____
      D. Romans 1:24_____
      E. Ephesians 5:5–6_____
      F. Revelation 21:27_____

3. *What must be my attitude toward the cross?*
  (1) Galatians 6:14_____
  (2) Mark 8:34_____
  (3) 1 Corinthians 1:18_____

4. *Learn the following verses:*
 Romans 6:23; Romans 5:8; 2 Corinthians 5:15

Study No. 7

IS CHRIST ALIVE NOW?
- God didn't leave Jesus dead;
- That would have been tragedy.

- He raised Him from the dead;
- That is victory!

List the sequence of events:

Luke 23:52–53_____

Matthew 28:2_____

Mark 16:6_____

HE IS RISEN!

1. *What are the evidences for His resurrection?*

    (1) What had Jesus predicted?

        A. Matthew 20: 18-19_____

        B. John 2:18–21_____

        C. John 11:25_____

    (2) What had the Old Testament prophesied?

        Psalm 16:10_____

    (3) Who saw Him after His resurrection?

        A. 1 Corinthians 15:5–8

            (a) _____ (d) _____

            (b) _____ (e) _____

            (c) _____ (f) _____

    (4) What happened to His body?

        Luke 24:2-3_____

    (5) What happened to the disciples?

        A. Compare Matthew 26:71–74 and Acts 2:14

        Before the resurrection, Peter_____

        After the resurrection, Peter_____

        B. Compare John 20:25 and John 20:28

_____

_____

        C. Compare Mark 14:50 and Acts 4:33

_____

_____

(6) What did Paul say?
    A. Acts 22:6–7_____
    B. Acts 26:15–16_____

2. *What are the results of His resurrection?*
    (1) For Christ
        A. Romans 1:4_____
        B. Colossians 1:18_____
        C. Acts 10:40-41_____
        D. Ephesians 1:20–21_____
    (2) For mankind
        A. Acts 24:15_____
        B. John 5:28–29_____
        C. Daniel 12:2_____
        D. Romans 14:9_____
    (3) For Christians
        A. Romans 4:25_____
        B. Romans 10:9_____
        C. Romans 5:10_____
        D. John 14:19_____
        E. 1 Thessalonians 4:14_____
        F. 1 Peter 1:3_____
        G. Romans 8:11_____

3. *What should be my experience of His resurrection?*
    (1) Colossians 2:12 (KJV)— "Ye are risen with Him . . .
    — raised with Him to a new life, sharing His
    resurrection life. Therefore, I must —
        A. Colossians 3:1_____
        B. Colossians 3:2_____
        C. Colossians 3:5_____
        D. Colossians 3:8_____

    E. Colossians 3:12_____

    F. Colossians 3:15

        (a)_____

        (b)_____

    G. Colossians 3:16_____

    H. Colossians 3:17_____

(2) Galatians 2:20 — The risen Christ lives in me.
Therefore, I should —

    A. Philippians 3:10_____

    B. Ephesians 1:18–19_____

    C. Galatians 2:8_____

4. *Learn the following verses:*
    Galatians 2:20;   Romans 10:9;   Colossians 2:12

Study No. 8

WHO IS THE HOLY SPIRIT?

    • God showed Himself generally in creation.

    • He revealed Himself particularly in Christ.

    • He reveals Himself personally in the Holy Spirit by coming to live with you.

1. *The Holy Spirit is a Person*

    (1) Which personal acts does He perform?

        A. John 14:17_____

        B. John 16:13

            (a)_____

            (b)_____

            (c)_____

            (d)_____

        C. Acts 13:2_____

        D. Acts 13:4_____

   (2) Which personal attributes does He display?

        A. 1 Corinthians 12:11_____

        B. Romans 8:27_____

        C. 1 Corinthians 2:13_____

        D. Romans 15:13_____

   (3) How did Christ speak of Him as a Person?

        A. John 14:16_____

        B. John 14:17

                (a)_____

                (b)_____

                (c)_____

                (d)_____

   (4) How is it possible to treat Him as a Person?

        A. Acts 5:3_____

        B. Acts 5:9_____

        C. Acts 7:51_____

        D. Ephesians 4:30_____

        E. Hebrews 10:29_____

2. *The Holy Spirit is God*

   (1) By which divine titles is He called?

        A. Genesis 6:3_____

        B. 2 Chronicles 15:1_____

        C. Isaiah 11:2_____

        D. Isaiah 61:1_____

        E. Matthew 10:20_____

        F. Romans 8:9_____

        G. Galatians 4:6_____

   (2) Which divine attributes does He display?

        A. Hebrews 9:14_____

        B. 1 John 5:6_____

    C. 1 Thessalonians 4:8_____

    D. Psalm 139:7–10_____

    E. 1 Corinthians 2:10_____

(3) Which divine tasks does He perform?

    A. Job 26:13 (NKJV)_____

    B. Matthew 12:28_____

    C. John 3:5_____

(4) In which great events did He participate?

    A. Genesis 1:2_____

    B. Matthew 1:18–20_____

    C. Luke 4:1_____

    D. Hebrews 9:14_____

    E. Romans 8:11_____

    F. 2 Peter 1:21_____

3. *What are the Holy Spirit's qualities?*

    A. Romans 1:4_____

    B. Isaiah 11:2

        (a)_____

        (b)_____

        (c)_____

        (d)_____

        (e)_____

        (f)_____

    C. Zechariah 12:10 (NKJV)_____

    D. John 14:17_____

    E. Romans 8:2_____

    F. Romans 8:15_____

    G. 2 Corinthians 4:13_____

    H. 2 Timothy 1:7

        (a)_____

        (b)_____

    (c)_____

I. Hebrews 10:29_____

J. 1 Peter 4:14_____

K. Isaiah 4:4

    (a)_____

    (b)_____

4. *What should be my experience of the Holy Spirit?*

I must be _____ of the Spirit (John 3:8) that I might _____ by the Spirit (Gal 5:25). If I _____ with the Spirit (5:25) day by day, I will not _____ (5:16).

If I refuse to yield to the Spirit living within me, I will _____ the Spirit (1 Thess. 5:19) and _____ the Spirit (Eph. 4:30). I must be continually _____with the Spirit (5:18) now that I have become a _____ for _____ by the Spirit (2:22). As I am _____ by the Spirit (Rom. 8:14) I will be _____ by the Spirit (Eph. 3:16). He will _____ (John 14:26) and I will be filled with _____ and _____ through the power of the Holy Spirit (Rom. 15:13).

5. *Learn the following verses*

  John 14:17;   Romans 8:26;   1 Peter 4:14

"Do your best to present yourself to God as one approved,[a] a worker who has no need to be ashamed, rightly handling the word of truth" 2 Timothy 2:15.

ENDNOTES

1. Miles, Alfred H. (Ed) *The Sacred Poets of the Nineteenth Century.* George Routledge & Sons; New York: E. P. Dutton & Co., 1907; Bartleby.com, 2011. www.bartleby.com/294/10. html. Accessed on July 1, 2013.

2. *"A General Confession."* The Book of Common Prayer (1928). http://justus.anglican.org/resources/bcp/1928/MP.htm. Accessed on July 1, 2013.

This book was produced by CLC Publications. We hope it has been life-changing and has given you a fresh experience of God through the work of the Holy Spirit. CLC Publications is an outreach of CLC Ministries International, a global literature mission with work in over fifty countries. If you would like to know more about us, we invite you to contact us at:

CLC Ministries International
PO Box 1449
Fort Washington, PA 19034

———————

E-mail: mail@clcusa.org
Website: www.clcpublications.com

— — — — — — — — — — — — — — — —

DO YOU LOVE GOOD CHRISTIAN BOOKS?
Do you have a heart for worldwide missions?

You can receive a FREE subscription to
CLC's newsletter on global literature missions
Order by e-mail at:

clcworld@clcusa.org

or mail your request to:

PO Box 1449
Fort Washington, PA 19034

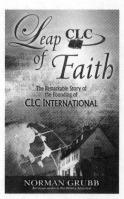

HOLINESS WITHOUT THE HALO

Stuart and Jill Briscoe

In this engaging book by Stuart and Jill Briscoe, you will discover that there is no conflict with being thoroughly happy, truly healthy, and practically holy. And you will also learn what God is asking of you when He says, "Be holy, because I am holy."

Trade Paper
Size 5¹/₄ x 8, Pages 224
ISBN: 978-1-936143-17-7
ISBN (*e-book*): 978-1-61958-004-6
$13.99
(*e-book*) - $9.99

TAKING GOD SERIOUSLY

Stuart Briscoe

Seasoned pastor Stuart Briscoe examines each of the Minor Prophets, providing both helpful historical context, and demonstrating the relevance of each prophet's message to believers today. If you want to take God's words from the Minor Prophets seriously, this book will help enrich your Bible study.

Trade Paper
Size 5¹/₄ x 8, Pages 208
ISBN: 978-1-61958-078-7
ISBN (*e-book*): 978-1-61958-079-4
$12.99
(*e-book*) - $9.99

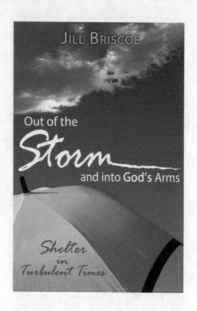

OUT OF THE STORM AND INTO GOD'S ARMS

Jill Briscoe

What do you do when the storm clouds of life surround you—and you can't see the silver lining? Where do you turn when God feels distant? Exploring truths from the book of Job, Jill Briscoe addresses the tough issues involved in the collision of affliction and faith.

Trade Paper
Size 5¼ x 8, Pages 208
ISBN: 978-1-61958-008-4
ISBN (*e-book*): 978-1-61958-021-3
$12.99
(*e-book*) - $9.99